First World War
and Army of Occupation
War Diary
France, Belgium and Germany

42 DIVISION
126 Infantry Brigade,
Brigade Trench Mortar Battery
26 March 1917 - 31 December 1918

WO95/2658/4

The Naval & Military Press Ltd
www.nmarchive.com
Published in association with The National Archives

Published by

The Naval & Military Press Ltd

Unit 10 Ridgewood Industrial Park,

Uckfield, East Sussex,

TN22 5QE England

Tel: +44 (0) 1825 749494

www.naval-military-press.com

www.nmarchive.com

This diary has been reprinted in facsimile from the original. Any imperfections are inevitably reproduced and the quality may fall short of modern type and cartographic standards.

© Crown Copyright
Images reproduced by permission of The National Archives, London, England, 2015.

Contents

Document type	Place/Title	Date From	Date To
Heading	WO95/2658 (4) 126 Inf Bgde Bgde Trench Mortar Battery April 17-Dec 18.		
Heading	42nd Division 126th Infy Bde Trench Mortar Batteries Apr 1917-Dec 1918.		
Heading	126th Trench Mortar Battery Volume I From March 26th To 31st 1917.		
War Diary	St Maxent	26/03/1917	30/03/1917
War Diary	Liercourt	31/03/1917	31/03/1917
Heading	126th Light Trench Mortar Battery Volume II From April 1st 1917 To April 30th 1917		
War Diary	Liercourt	01/04/1917	07/04/1917
War Diary	Morcourt	08/04/1917	11/04/1917
War Diary	Frise	12/04/1917	17/04/1917
War Diary	Peronne.	18/04/1917	18/04/1917
War Diary	Langavesnes.	19/04/1917	20/04/1917
War Diary	Longavesnes And Villers Fancon.	21/04/1917	22/04/1917
War Diary	Villers Faucon and Epehy.	23/04/1917	29/04/1917
War Diary	Villers Faucon and Longavesnes.	30/04/1917	30/04/1917
Heading	126th Light Trench Mortar Battery Volume III. From May 1st 1917 To May 31st 1917.		
War Diary	Longavesnes.	01/05/1917	05/05/1917
War Diary	St Emelie and Lempire	06/05/1917	16/05/1917
War Diary	St Emelie Lempire & Longavesnes.	17/05/1917	17/05/1917
War Diary	Longavesnes.	18/05/1917	18/05/1917
War Diary	Longavesnes and Equancourt (Camp VII.a)	19/05/1917	19/05/1917
War Diary	Camp. V. II. d. & Neuville.	20/05/1917	20/05/1917
War Diary	Neuville-Bourjonval.	20/05/1917	20/05/1917
War Diary	Neuville Bourjonval and P.18.d.3.1 Sheet 57c.	21/05/1917	21/05/1917
War Diary	P.18.d.3.1. & Trescault.	22/05/1917	31/05/1917
Heading	126th Light Trench Mortar Battery Volume IV From June 1st To June 30th 1917.		
War Diary	Trescault and P.18.d.5.2.	01/06/1917	02/06/1917
War Diary	Trescault P.18.d.5.2 "Q" B.5.3.	03/06/1917	03/06/1917
War Diary	Trescault Q 14.b. 5.3.	04/06/1917	21/06/1917
War Diary	Ytres.	22/06/1917	27/06/1917
War Diary	Ytres and Havrincourt Wood (Q.14.b.5.3)	28/06/1917	30/06/1917
Heading	126th Light Trench Mortar Battery. War Diary July 1917 Volume V.		
Heading	126th Light Trench Mortar Battery Volume V From July 1st 1917 To July 31st 1917.		
War Diary	Trescault and Q 14 b. 5.3.	01/07/1917	08/07/1917
War Diary	Barastre.	08/07/1917	08/07/1917
War Diary	Barastre & Bihucourt.	09/07/1917	09/07/1917
War Diary	Bihucourt.	10/07/1917	10/07/1917
War Diary	Bihucourt & Courcelles.	11/07/1917	11/07/1917
War Diary	Courcelles.	12/07/1917	31/07/1917
Miscellaneous	Orders by Capt H.J. Hampson O.C. 176 L.M.B.	07/07/1917	07/07/1917
Heading	126th Light Trench Mortar Battery Volume VI August 1st 1917 To August 31st 1917.		
War Diary	Courcelles.	01/08/1917	20/08/1917

Type	Location	From	To
War Diary	Courcelles & Bertrancourt.	21/08/1917	22/08/1917
War Diary	Trappistes.	23/08/1917	30/08/1917
War Diary	Ypres.	30/08/1917	31/08/1917
Heading	126th Light Trench Mortar Battery. Volume VII From Sept 1st 1917 To Sept 30th 1917.		
War Diary	Ypres.	01/09/1917	16/09/1917
War Diary	Bedouin Camp (Brandhock)	16/09/1917	18/09/1917
War Diary	Winnezeele.	19/09/1917	20/09/1917
War Diary	Wormhoudt.	21/09/1917	21/09/1917
War Diary	Tetegham.	27/09/1917	27/09/1917
War Diary	La Panne.	23/09/1917	23/09/1917
War Diary	Coxyde Bains.	24/09/1917	30/09/1917
Heading	126th Light Trench Mortar Battery. Volume VIII. From Oct. 1st 1917 To Oct 31st 1917.		
War Diary	Coxyde Bains.	01/10/1917	05/10/1917
War Diary	Nieuport.	06/10/1917	31/10/1917
Heading	126th Light Trench Motar Battery Volume IX. From Nov 1st 1917 To Nov 30th 1917.		
War Diary	Nieuport.	01/11/1917	18/11/1917
War Diary	Oost-Dunkerke and Wormhoudt.	19/11/1917	19/11/1917
War Diary	Wormhoudt.	19/11/1917	20/11/1917
War Diary	Staple Area.	21/11/1917	21/11/1917
War Diary	Warne.	22/11/1917	26/11/1917
War Diary	Molinghem.	27/11/1917	27/11/1917
War Diary	Bethune.	28/11/1917	30/11/1917
Heading	126th Light Trench Mortar Battery. Volume X From 1st Dec. 1917 To 31st Dec 1917.		
War Diary	Bethune.	01/12/1917	10/12/1917
War Diary	Le Preol.	11/12/1917	31/12/1917
Heading	126th Light Trench Mortar Battery Volume XI From Jan 1st 1918 To Jan 31st 1918.		
War Diary	Le Preol	01/01/1918	04/01/1918
War Diary	Beuvry	05/01/1918	17/01/1918
War Diary	Festubert	18/01/1918	21/01/1918
War Diary	Gorre (F4a 60.17)	22/01/1918	31/01/1918
Heading	126th Light Trench Mortar Battery Volume XII From Feb 1st 1918 To Feb 28th 1918.		
War Diary	Gorre.	01/02/1918	04/02/1918
Miscellaneous	Headquarters, 42nd. Division. B.M.C.22/71.	05/03/1918	05/03/1918
War Diary	Gorre.	05/02/1918	14/02/1918
War Diary	Gorre and Busnes.	14/02/1918	17/02/1918
War Diary	Busnes	18/02/1918	28/02/1918
Heading	42nd Division. 126th Infantry Brigade. 126th Light Trench Mortar Battery March 1918		
Heading	126th Light Trench Mortar Battery Volume XIII From March 1st 1918 To March 31st 1918.		
War Diary	Busnes.	01/03/1918	03/03/1918
War Diary	Busnes & Burbure.	04/03/1918	04/03/1918
War Diary	Burbure.	05/03/1918	23/03/1918
War Diary	Adinfer Wood.	23/03/1918	24/03/1918
War Diary	Logeast Wood	24/03/1918	24/03/1918
War Diary	Railway Cutting N' Courcelles	25/03/1918	25/03/1918
War Diary	Ablainzeville.	26/03/1918	27/03/1918
War Diary	Essarts Les Bucquoy	27/03/1918	31/03/1918
Operation(al) Order(s)	Battery Operation Order No. 34.	03/03/1919	03/03/1919

Operation(al) Order(s)	Administrations Instructions In Accordance With O.O. No. 34.	08/03/1918	08/03/1918
Heading	126th Inf. Bde. 42nd Div. War Diary 126th Light Trench Mortar Battery. April 1918.		
Heading	126th Light Trench Mortar Battery Volume XIV From April 1st 1918 To April 30th 1918		
War Diary	Essarts Les Bucquoy.	01/04/1918	04/04/1918
War Diary	Pigeon Wood.	05/04/1918	06/04/1918
War Diary	Souastre.	07/04/1918	07/04/1918
War Diary	Henu.	08/04/1918	15/04/1918
War Diary	Line Hqrs Gommecourt Wood.	16/04/1918	30/04/1918
Heading	Appendices.		
Operation(al) Order(s)	Battery Operation Order No. 35.	03/04/1918	03/04/1918
Operation(al) Order(s)	Battery Operation Order No. 36.	06/04/1918	06/04/1918
Operation(al) Order(s)	Battery Operation Order No. 37	07/04/1918	07/04/1918
Operation(al) Order(s)	Battery Operation Order No. 38.	15/04/1918	15/04/1918
Miscellaneous	Issued With Battery Operation Order No. 38.	15/04/1918	15/04/1918
Operation(al) Order(s)	Battery Operation Order No. 39.	18/04/1918	18/04/1918
Operation(al) Order(s)	Relief Table In accordance with Battery O.O. No. 39.		
Operation(al) Order(s)	Battery Operation Order No. 40	22/04/1918	22/04/1918
Operation(al) Order(s)	Relief table in accordance with Battery O.O. No. 40.		
Operation(al) Order(s)	Battery Operation Order No. 41.	25/04/1918	25/04/1918
Operation(al) Order(s)	Relief table in accordance with Battery O.O. No. 41.	25/04/1918	25/04/1918
Operation(al) Order(s)	Battery Operation Order No. 42.	30/04/1918	30/04/1918
Operation(al) Order(s)	Relief table in accordance with Battery O.O. No 42.		
Miscellaneous	Inf Bde.	01/06/1918	01/06/1918
Heading	126th Light Trench Mortar Battery Volume XV From May 1st 1918 To May 31st 1918		
War Diary	Line Hqrs Gommecourt Wood.	01/05/1918	02/05/1918
War Diary	Bayencourt	03/05/1918	06/05/1918
War Diary	Pas Woods (C.17.d).	07/05/1918	09/05/1918
War Diary	Pas Woods.	16/05/1918	31/05/1918
Operation(al) Order(s)	Battery Operation Order No 43.	01/05/1918	01/05/1918
Operation(al) Order(s)	Battery Operation Order No 44	05/05/1918	05/05/1918
Miscellaneous		05/05/1918	05/05/1918
Heading	126th Light Trench Mortar Battery Volume XVI. From June 1st 1918 To June 30th 1918.		
War Diary	Pas Woods (C.17.d.3.3)	01/06/1918	06/06/1918
War Diary	Pas Woods (C.17.d.33) and J.24.d.66.38 (Batty Hqrs)	07/06/1918	07/06/1918
War Diary	Line Batty Hqrs J.24.D.66.38.	08/06/1918	23/06/1918
War Diary	Bus Woods	24/06/1918	30/06/1918
Heading	126th Light Trench Mortar Battery War Diary Volume XVII From 1st July 1918 To 31st July 1918.		
War Diary	Bus.	01/07/1918	02/07/1918
War Diary	Line Battery Hqrs. (K.25.b.0.5).	03/07/1918	08/07/1918
War Diary	Battery Hqrs J.24.c.9.8.	09/07/1918	18/07/1918
War Diary	Bus Wood	19/07/1918	26/07/1918
War Diary	Battery Hqrs. P.5.a.70.70.	27/07/1918	31/07/1918
War Diary	Fort Bertha.	01/08/1918	13/08/1918
War Diary	Bus Woods	13/08/1918	19/08/1918
War Diary	Bertrancourt	20/08/1918	21/08/1918
War Diary	Fort Stewart.	22/08/1918	23/08/1918
War Diary	Fort Stewart (K.20.b).	24/08/1918	25/08/1918
War Diary	Little Wood (M.9.d.9.8).	26/08/1918	30/08/1918
War Diary	La Barque and Pys.	31/08/1918	31/08/1918

Type	Description	From	To
Heading	126th Light Trench Mortar Battery. War Diary Volume XIX From Sept 1st 1918 To Sept 30th 1918.		
War Diary	Pys	01/09/1918	04/09/1918
War Diary	Villers-Au-Flos.	03/09/1918	06/09/1918
War Diary	Luisenhof Farm.	07/09/1918	20/09/1918
War Diary	I.29.b.0.3.	20/09/1918	21/09/1918
War Diary	Battery Hqrs.	22/09/1918	22/09/1918
War Diary	Q.14.b.8.5.	22/09/1918	28/09/1918
War Diary	Q.14.b.2.6.	29/09/1918	30/09/1918
Heading	War Diary 126th Light Trench Mortar Battery. Volume XX From Oct 1st 1918 To Oct 31st 1918.		
War Diary	Havrincourt Wood (Q.14.b.2.6).	01/10/1918	09/10/1918
War Diary	Briseux Wood. (N.10.C.0.S).	10/10/1918	10/10/1918
War Diary	Fontaine Au Pere.	11/10/1918	11/10/1918
War Diary	Aulicourt Farm.	12/10/1918	18/10/1918
War Diary	Prayelle.	18/10/1918	21/10/1918
War Diary	Aulicourt Farm.	22/10/1918	23/10/1918
War Diary	Beauvois.	24/10/1918	31/10/1918
Heading	126th Light Trench Mortar Battery. War Diary Volume XXI From 1st Nov 1918 To 30th Novr 1918.		
War Diary	Beauvois.	01/11/1918	03/11/1918
War Diary	Solesmes.	04/11/1918	04/11/1918
War Diary	Beaudignies.	05/11/1918	05/11/1918
War Diary	N.20.a.4.3.	06/11/1918	07/11/1918
War Diary	O.37.b.3.8.	08/11/1918	08/11/1918
War Diary	Hautmont.	09/11/1918	30/11/1918
Operation(al) Order(s)	Operation Order No. 75.	03/11/1918	03/11/1918
Operation(al) Order(s)	Operation Order No. 76.	07/11/1918	07/11/1918
Operation(al) Order(s)	Battery Order No. 77.	30/11/1918	30/11/1918
Heading	126th Light Trench Mortar Battery War Diary Volume XXII From Decr 1st 1918 To Decr 31st 1918.		
War Diary	Hautmont.	01/12/1918	14/12/1918
War Diary	Lamories.	15/12/1918	15/12/1918
War Diary	Binche.	16/12/1918	16/12/1918
War Diary	Fontaine L'Eveque.	17/12/1918	18/12/1918
War Diary	Gilly.	19/12/1918	31/12/1918
Operation(al) Order(s)	Battery Order No. 78.	12/12/1918	12/12/1918
Miscellaneous	March Table Starting point.		
Operation(al) Order(s)	Administrative Instruction issued with Battery Order No. 78	12/12/1918	12/12/1918
Miscellaneous	Battery Area.		

WO95/2658 (4)

126 INF BGDE
BGDE TRENCH MORTAR BATTERY
Apr '17 — Dec '18

42ND DIVISION
126TH INFY BDE

TRENCH MORTAR BATTERIES
APR 1917-DEC 1918

42ND DIVISION
126TH INFY BDE

Army Form C. 2118.

WAR DIARY
or
INTELLIGENCE SUMMARY
(Erase heading not required.)

Duplicate

126th Trench Mortar Battery

Volume I

From March 26th to 31st 1917

Army Form C. 2118.

WAR DIARY
or
INTELLIGENCE SUMMARY
(Erase heading not required.)

Duplicate

Instructions regarding War Diaries and Intelligence Summaries are contained in F. S. Regs., Part II. and the Staff Manual respectively. Title Pages will be prepared in manuscript.

Place	Date	Hour	Summary of Events and Information	Remarks and references to Appendices
St Maxent	26/3/17		Arrived in St Maxent & took over billets	
"	27/3/17		Training. The scheme made for the rapid movement of Mortars	
"	28/3/17		Training. Billets taken in advance in Lorcourt	
"	29/3/17		Training. Lecture by Divisional Gas Officer	
"	30/3/17		Marched to Lorcourt & took over billets	
Lorcourt	31/3/17		Training. Nothing to report	

H A O'Brien Capt
O.C. 126 L.M. Batt

WAR DIARY
or
INTELLIGENCE SUMMARY.
(Erase heading not required.)

Army Form C. 2118.

126th Light Trench Mortar Battery

Volume II

From April 1st 1917 to April 30th 1917.

Reference Maps.

Abbeville 14   1/100.000
Amiens 17   1/100.000
62c N.E.   1/20.000
57c S.E.   1/20.000

Army Form C. 2118.

WAR DIARY
or
INTELLIGENCE SUMMARY.
(Erase heading not required.)

Place	Date	Hour	Summary of Events and Information	Remarks and references to Appendices
LIERCOURT	1/4/17		Training. Nothing to report. MM.	
"	2/4/17		Ams Insp. Inspection of quarters by A.B.C. MM.	
"	3/4/17		Training. 20 men detailed to Brigade for training purposes. MM.	
"	4/4/17		Training. 12 trucks were made available for training purposes. Billets taken over at FONTAINE near " for more available. MM.	
"	5/4/17		Training. Orders regarding move received. MM.	
"	6/4/17		Training. Extra baggage sent by train from PONT REMY. Change at Ailly sur Noye. MM	
"	7/4/17		Marched to PONT REMY & entrained. Detrained at La FLAQUE & marched to MORCOURT where billets were taken over in camp. MM.	
MORCOURT	8/4/17		Nothing to report. MM	
"	9/4/17		Training. Nothing to report. MM	
"	10/4/17		Training. Orders received for move. MM	
"	11/4/17		Marched to FRISE and took over billets. MM	
FRISE	12/4/17		Training. Conference at H.Q. with reference to march discipline etc. MM	
"	13/4/17		Training. Relieved by 2/5th Manchesters. MM	
"	14/4/17		Movement. Scouts and snipers taken over from 9th Manchesters. Relieve 6.4 to start ... MM	

WAR DIARY or INTELLIGENCE SUMMARY

Army Form C. 2118.

(Erase heading not required.)

Place	Date	Hour	Summary of Events and Information	Remarks and references to Appendices
FRISE	15/4/17		Training. Orders received for move. Nothing else to report. MM	
"	16/4/17		Runway. Transport etc. loaded in advance. Marched off to B.M.D. Special instructions for M.O.'s in company work. MM	
"	17/4/17		Marched to Peronne and took over billets from 125 I.M. Factory. Arrangements made regarding F.W. "inside start" barometers that were immediately brought out of the line by the 125 Brigade. MM	
PERONNE	18/4/17		Marched to LONGAVESNES and carried light work. W/ M/c 3 M.Gunny H/M	
LONGAVESNES	19/4/17		Superior station emplacement in the BROWN LINE. Field worked. M.1-3 T.M.D. MM	
"	20/4/17		Attached were return to their battalion. A small mine exploded at the road junction E 35 d 79 at about 9.30 pm holding the M.O. of the 10th M.R. MM	
			Marched to VILLERS FAUCON and took over billets from m.3 T.M. Battery. Relieved them in the "BROWN LINE". The road between EPEHY and SAULCOURT lightly shelled. Work carried out on improvement of billet at EPEHY and VILLERS FAUCON. MM	
LONGAVESNES → VILLERS FAUCON.	21/4/17			
	22/4/17		Defences emplacement commenced on the Brown line. Work carried out on fresh quarters for the section on that line. EPEHY shelled during morning about 10.30 am. MM	

Army Form C. 2118.

Instructions regarding War Diaries and Intelligence Summaries are contained in F. S. Regs., Part II. and the Staff Manual respectively. Title pages will be prepared in manuscript.

WAR DIARY
or
INTELLIGENCE SUMMARY.

(Erase heading not required.)

Army Form C. 2118.

Place	Date	Hour	Summary of Events and Information	Remarks and references to Appendices
VILLERS FAUCON DEPEHY	22/4/17		Two Stokes guns attached to the 14th West Kents Regt and moved up and that went to QUARRY (X.29.d.2.3. Sheet 57 C.S.E.) Temporary defensive emplacements constructed.	
"	24/4/17		A third mortar took up its "BROWN LINE". No firing done by any of these guns. MM. Gun in QUARRY withdrawn to "BROWN LINE". To consolidate positions by the Battery MM.	
"	25/4/17		No. 2 Section relieved No. 1 Section in the "BROWN LINE". Work continued on defensive emplacements. Also small R.E. fatigues. MM.	
"	26/4/17		Both continued on "BROWN LINE". Both sections of the Battery used for R.E. fatigue under Major Gleave, R.E. MM.	
"	27/4/17		Fresh emplacements and gun stores for guns in "BROWN LINE". Interview with Brigadier General regarding position of Stokes Guns in advance outposts MM.	
"	28/4/17		Ammunition carried by the 116th Machine Regt collected to and by Battery work continued on "BROWN LINE" defences + quarters. Advance party of 1,2,3,4,5 NB arrived at VILLERS FAUCON. Large fire at ST EMELIE during the night. MM.	
"	29/4/17		No. 1 Section relieved No. 2 Section in the "BROWN LINE" and continued the work in progress. Advance party sent on to PERONNE early in the day was recalled owing to alteration in Operation Orders. MM.	
VILLERS FAUCON and LONGAVESNES	30/4/17		Advance party sent on to LONGAVESNES, to take over billets. 127 L.T.M.B. took over our billets at VILLERS FAUCON and relieved the section in the "BROWN LINE" the Battery marched to LONGAVESNES and took over billets there MM.	

H. P. Morein Capt.
O.C. 126 & L.T.M. 13 Batt

Confidential

WAR DIARY
or
INTELLIGENCE SUMMARY.

(*Erase heading not required.*)

Army Form C. 2118.

126th Light Trench Mortar Battery.

Volume III

From May 1st 1917 to May 31st 1917

WAR DIARY
or
INTELLIGENCE SUMMARY

Army Form C. 2118.

Place	Date	Hour	Summary of Events and Information	Remarks and references to Appendices
LONGUENESSE	1/5/17		Besses on fatigue for Town Major. Conference at BHQ at 5pm. AAA	
"	2/5/17		Battery on fatigue for Town Major. AAA	
"	3/5/17		Cook Parade. Gas alarm lab at night. All over AAA	
"	4/5/17		Arranged regarding taking over on the line from 122 & 175 T.M.B. AAA	
"	5/5/17		R.H. & party from H/5 T.M.R. Battery/s on N.S. to F.M.B. advanced gun positions. Also front line on extreme R.H. in LEMPIRE (?) advanced positions & reported latter. Gun positions. AAA	
"			R.H. of K[ ] from [ ] rest of them reported LIMPELE that bombardment on P.O. & B. AAA	
SIEMELIE and LEMPIRE	6/5/17 4.15pm		Moved Hqrs to LIMPELE. Trenches in very dirty & untidy condition & no posts B. AAA	
"	7/5/17		Continued working on emplacements & on post B. Q2 Guns and 138 rounds taken up. Retaliation very slight. AAA	
"	8/5/17 10pm		Kept the round conflicts in post B. 16 casualties. No. 2 section relieved No. 1 sec the line. Nothing broken. 108 rounds fired AAA	
"	9/5/17		Carrying party returned to Agis. AAA	
"	10/5/17		Conference at B.H.Q. Reconnaissance made on right gatt. front. AAA	
"	11/5/17		Continuation of work on emplacement. AAA	
"	12/5/17		Carrying party from Boreyet Regt. LEMPIRE took stokes shells and bombs to the line. AAA	
"	13/5/17		Bre Gen E. Steke Wells taken to right Batt. Headquarters. AAA	

WAR DIARY
or
INTELLIGENCE SUMMARY.
(Erase heading not required.)

Army Form C. 2118.

Place	Date	Hour	Summary of Events and Information	Remarks and references to Appendices
SEMELIE	14/5/17		No.2 Section relieved No.1. in the line. One gun and 50 rounds Stokes Ammunition taken to Battalion H.Q (F.23.c.0.1.) Work commenced on gun emplacement + Ammn. recess.	
LEMPIRE	15/5/17		Reconnaissance made round GILLEMONT FARM. Construction of gun emplacement and ammunition recess.	
"	16/5/17		Orders received to move to LONGAVESNES. Gun emplacement + Ammn recess completed at F.23.c.0.7.	
SEMELIE LEMPIRE + LONGAVESNES	17/5/17		Advanced party proceeds to LONGAVESNES. Men with line worked on undercoating and improving sheds. All Stokes shells taken from LEMPIRE by 1 Limber and 1 G.S. wagon. 36 rounds handed over to D.A.C. Remaining 111 rounds taken to Batt. H.Q. LONGAVESNES.	
LONGAVESNES	18/5/17	4:00 am	No.2 Section moved from the line to Batt. H.Q. Operation orders received to march to new area + relief of 5th Brigade. Men reclothed in the afternoon + cleaned up equipment, clothing and hand carts. Advanced party of 1 N.C.O. + 1 N.C.O. proceeded to EQUANCOURT to take over bivouacs. Capt. Humphries reported for duty + took over command of the Battery.	
LONGAVESNES	19/5/17	5:30 am	Battery moved to new area + arrived at Camp V.11.a at 9:45 am.	
and EQUANCOURT	"	12 noon	Conference at B.A.Q. H.Q.	
(Map V.11.a) (CAMPV.11.a	20/5/17		Voluntary church parade at 9:30 am. Stand-to's cleaned + inspected. Advanced party proceeds to NEUVILLE-BOURJONVAL and took over from 127 L.T.M.Battery. The Battery	
NEUVILLE	"			

… Army Form C. 2118.

WAR DIARY
or
INTELLIGENCE SUMMARY.
(Erase heading not required.)

Place	Date	Hour	Summary of Events and Information	Remarks and references to Appendices
NEUVILLE BOURJONVAL	20/5/17		Moved to NEUVILLE-BOURJONVAL at 5.0pm and arrived there 6.0pm. Capt Hairson and 5. O.R. went up to the line to inspect front positions. JM	
NEUVILLE- BOURJONVAL	21/5/17	9.0am 5.30pm	Bath inspection at 9.0am. Kit inspection at 10.0am. Operation orders & administrative orders received regarding relief of 50th L.T.M.B. (20th Divn.) JM The Battery moved to P.18.d.3.1 (sheet 57) Holt's Sun.	
And P.18.d.3.1 Sheet 57 P.18.d.3.1 & TRESCAULT	22/5/17		Relief was completed without casualties at 12 to 4 a.m. Took over from 51st Tr.M. Battery (HARINCOURT FRONT) Men worked on cleaning shells, trench fatigues. Conference at 115th Inf Bn HQrs at 2.30pm JM	
"	23/5/17		Men in the huts worked on improving emplacements. Men at Batty HQ continued work on cleaning shells, water fatigues & gun instruction. Col. Murray White at 6.0pm at Battalion HQ with reference to enemy trench mortars. 17 bombs (23 L Round Stokes Shells) were taken to Section HQrs by Bombs At 9.25 & 9.43 the German were given by means of the Stoken Storming JM	
"	24/5/17		Work carried on as before in gun positions. Enemy fatigue round camps for men at P18.d.3.1. The left centre sub sections were relieved by men in reserve. The relieving party took with them 17 (Boxes) 5 Medium Bombard Vavendes to be evenly distributed between the left & centre sub section guns. JM	
"	25/5/17	2.0am	The party placed 6 rounds at P.18.d.3.1. The men had a bath at METZ during the afternoon. Capt Hairson and 2.M. M. Hewitt	

A.5834 Wt W.4975/M687 750,000 8/16 D. D. & L. Ltd. Forms/C.2118/13

Army Form C. 2118.

WAR DIARY
or
INTELLIGENCE SUMMARY.
(Erase heading not required.)

Place	Date	Hour	Summary of Events and Information	Remarks and references to Appendices

WAR DIARY
or
INTELLIGENCE SUMMARY.

Army Form C. 2118.

Place	Date	Hour	Summary of Events and Information	Remarks and references to Appendices
O 18 A 31 a 3	2/5/17		Wire reconnoitred from position chosen for defence barrage work. Enemy machine gun (50 yds left of new German MG emplacement @ O 4 c 67-59) opened fire & made reptiles action.	
PRESCHOOT	3/5/17		Working party from Regt. proceeded to advance dump & not informed too late. Zero hour (11:00 pm & 1:00 am) bombardment on German position. Trench Mortar much firing to cover our attack by enemy. No Trench Mortar action on our action.	

M.J. Hampson Capt.
OC 156 T.M. Bty.

Army Form C. 2118.

WAR DIARY
or
INTELLIGENCE SUMMARY.
(Erase heading not required.)

196th Light Trench Mortar Battery

Volume IV

From June 1st to June 30th 1917.

Army Form C. 2118.

WAR DIARY
or
INTELLIGENCE SUMMARY.
(Erase heading not required.)

Place	Date	Hour	Summary of Events and Information	Remarks and references to Appendices
TRESCAULT P.18.d.5.2.	16/6/17		Working party from Battery Hqrs proceeded to Beaten Hqrs. to work done owing to operations. Fire from Enemy on the right position relieved by two teams of the 178.T.M.B which completed by 11. 30 a.m. without casualties.	Rgf. B.O. 61
"	2 P.M.		Working party sent from Headquarters asked for ammunition carrying. Forward posts found out in left battalion and right battalion front. Possibility of enemy observation but only on one mortar to be covered up. Battery to [illegible] in M.C.G. returned to Brigade Hqrs for instructions on the strength of the [illegible].	
TRESCAULT P.18.d.5.2. Q.W. K.5.3.	26/6/17		Having Nyo moved from S.Gd. K.5.3. two teak [illegible] [illegible] [illegible] by [illegible] of the battery. Good observation gained about 11. 30 a.m.	
TRESCAULT Q.W. K.5.3.	27/6/17		Working party from D.C.D to set Hqrs. to carry on work on mess shelter 30. N/A	
"	29/6/17		1.P.M. set men from each battalion on the Brigade refuge at Rosary Farm and attached to the rest [illegible] the duty. At 7.30 p.m. 1st Brigade F.O. L and Hilbert 2nd George at 1000 I left the Battery to open Mess went. N/A	

Army Form C. 2118.

WAR DIARY
or
INTELLIGENCE SUMMARY.
(Erase heading not required.)

Instructions regarding War Diaries and Intelligence Summaries are contained in F.S. Regs., Part II. and the Staff Manual respectively. Title pages will be prepared in manuscript.

Place	Date	Hour	Summary of Events and Information	Remarks and references to Appendices
TRESCAULT 4.O.L.L.53	6/6/19		Brent visited the men of the H.Q.C. 1st Brigade at 10.0 a.m. The Battery not relieved owing to the 125 & T.M.B. guns on a course to the Trench Army School of Mortars. Lt. McMillan returned up the Battery at Delm. Myr. Seven Gunners also returned to man from Battery Myr. DM	
"	7/6/19		Men in camp worked on dug outs for Battery Myr. Fairly peaceful. DM	
"	8/6/19		Lehm. Myr. to work on gun emplacement. 90th. Air alarms (more Zep.) at 1 & 2 a.m.	
"	9/6/19		During the day men worked on bedson dug outs for Battery Myr. no mortars fire. Hostile proceeded to point mortars in the line trenches or emplacements some at D6.	
"	10/6/19		Men worked on men dug outs during the day, also brought forms gun emplacement to Delm. Myr. to continue work on emplacement there. One man Lt. No.13 at Delm. Myr. got wounded by machine gun fire. DM	
"	11/6/19		Work continued on dug out at Battery Myr. All guns taken forward to temporary position at Delm. 18 rounds fires in retaliation for Germans	

WAR DIARY or INTELLIGENCE SUMMARY

Army Form C. 2118.

Place	Date	Hour	Summary of Events and Information	Remarks and references to Appendices
TRESCAULT (M10 b 3)			Started work on Dug Out. 90M	
	11/6/17		Continuation of work on dug out at Battery Hqrs. 2/Lt H.B. Deney relieved 2/Lt McMichael at Section Hqrs. Gun team relieved by men from Battery Hqrs. The gun was taken forward to a position and left to fire on fixed lines. [SHROPSHIRE SPUR] Nine rounds were fired. 90M	
	12/6/17		Men in camp worked on dug outs at Battery Hqrs. A gun was taken forward to a slab ready to fire. 90M	
	13/6/17		Work continued on Hqrs dug out. Working party proceeded to the line & carried ammunition and commenced a dug out in Coy. Sgt. Major's dug out 16 issues. Target being PENNY WOOD. NW × E of SHROPSHIRE SPUR. Total rounds fired. 60. 90M	
	14/6/17		Work continued on men's Hqrs dug out. The gun on Flap ford's 10 rounds. The gun on Flap ford's 10 twenty. 90M	
	15/6/17		275 rounds Stokes Ammunition taken up to dot Hqrs to replace defective fuses. Men worked on carrying ammunition 90M	
	16/6/17		Men in camp worked on dug out. 2/Lt W.H. Stewart relieved 2/Lt H.B. Deney at _____ 90M	

Army Form C. 2118.

WAR DIARY
or
INTELLIGENCE SUMMARY.
(Erase heading not required.)

Place	Date	Hour	Summary of Events and Information	Remarks and references to Appendices
RESGHAULT and 14y 6:53.	17/6/17		When mentioned work on dug out at Battery Agn. The gun teams are de-loused were exercised by Subaltern from Agn. by Lieut. Morton one from M Sub. (U.M.F. 45-70) and one from W Sub. 65.40 fired on enemy advanced line entrance of FAUX WOOD (N.4.25.76) and another edge of FAUX WOOD) and one end Q.M. Sgt K.D.P. C/Sgt. B. Sgt (W) Sgt L. Cpl. & 1 N.C.O. M.G. Retaliation. Lt Patterson and 3 O.Rs. returned from the III Corps school musketry.	
	18/6/17		Lt Patterson returned to M.M. school at Bolsom Agri.	
	19/6/17		Early practice did shaw for not made ammunition from Wagenuir. Observation orders received for the relief of the Battery by 125 K.M.A. M/A Batry.	
	20/6/17		Orders received for firmer relief to the night of 21/6/2. Nothing fresh. Proceeded to Belsian Agro Reference to a (firm fest command). M/A	
	21/6/17		Operation a demonstrative over recond sup. offence to the relief of the 125 Bde R.J. BO. 81 Capt. Selous Major opened the 125 M.B. went into waggon line left Station moved up taking over gun positions in the line. At 635 2M Battery moved out of gun line and took gun position in the Line. The relief of the 125 Battery by C/Battalion (125 Batty — Sicion arrived)	

Army Form C. 2118.

WAR DIARY
or
INTELLIGENCE SUMMARY.
(Erase heading not required.)

Instructions regarding War Diaries and Intelligence Summaries are contained in F. S. Regs., Part II. and the Staff Manual respectively. Title pages will be prepared in manuscript.

Place	Date	Hour	Summary of Events and Information	Remarks and references to Appendices
CAMP E53 YPRES	21/6/17		The battery on relief took over camp at YPRES evacuated by 183. DTMB.	DJM
YPRES	22/6/17		The men rested in the morning. In the afternoon drew up new clothing equipment. 2nd MTR trunk attached to XcO Ambulance with Saphie.	DJM
"	23/6/17		Orders received for the return to their numerous MCO who do well belong to the 43 Div. At 9 a.m. Rifle Sight Inspection. Football in the afternoon.	DJM
"	24/6/17		Continuation of training. Lecture on gas, gas drill squad Drill in the morning. Football in the afternoon.	DJM
"	25/6/17		Orders received for the relief of 183. L.T.M.B. by 126 L.T.M.B. Squad Drill, ceremonial drill, bayonet fighting in the morning. In the afternoon training of attached men in gun team work. Remainder digging emplacements. 4 NCO's and 1 O.R. proceeded to rejoin their unit, and struck off the strength of the Battery.	DJM
"	26/6/17		Close order Drill, Gas Helmet Drill, Bayonet fighting in the morning. Continuation of training of attached men in gun team work, digging emplacement in the afternoon. The baths at BERTINCOURT were placed at our disposal from noon to 1.30pm + all the men had a bath change.	DJM

Army Form C. 2118.

WAR DIARY
or
INTELLIGENCE SUMMARY.
(Erase heading not required.)

Place	Date	Hour	Summary of Events and Information	Remarks and references to Appendices
YPRES.	27/6/17		The Artillery were on the return of 125 L.T.M.B. to 17 L.T.M.B.	R/BO 88
YPRES	28/6/17		The daily training programme carried out.	
HAVRINCOURT WOOD (Q14.b.5.3)			The Battery moved at 2.0 pm from YPRES to HAVRINCOURT WOOD (Q14.b.5.3) and took over Mortars from 125 L.T.M.B. At dusk a party proceeded to the line and relieved the gun teams of 125 L.T.M.B. The relief was complete without casualties.	
"	29/6/17		Stokes Mortar in R.h.4.b fired 6 rounds at 2.30 am at the Eastern Edge of FEMY WOOD. " - E Sap fired 6 rounds at 2.15 - on the road by Elephants hut on SHROPSHIRE SPUR. Working party proceeded to Section H.Qrs & deliver water and sandbags from HQ Stores.	
"	30/6/17		A Stoke Mortar fired 15 rounds from F Sap on the EAST side of Quarry Carries in A 33.C.90.75.	

A.S.834 Wt. W4973/M687 750,000 8/16 D.D. & L. Ltd. Forms/C.2118/13

Confidential

(6202) W 11186/M1151 350,000 12/16 McA. & W., Ltd. (Est. 731) Forms/W 3091/3.   Army Form W. 3091.

Cover for Documents.

126th Light Trench Mortar Battery.

Nature of Enclosures.

War Diary

July 1917

Volume V

Notes, or Letters written.

Army Form C. 2118.

WAR DIARY
or
INTELLIGENCE SUMMARY.

(Erase heading not required.)

126th Light Trench Mortar Battery

Volume V

From July 1st 1917 to July 31st 1917.

WAR DIARY
INTELLIGENCE SUMMARY.
(Erase heading not required.)

Army Form C. 2118.

Place	Date	Hour	Summary of Events and Information	Remarks and references to Appendices
TRESCAULT and Ref. I.53	1/7/17		4 Stokes Mortars fired 20 rounds from E. Lab, the target being the road running from Ribécourt to K.H.a.70. Another mortar fired 20 rounds on SHROPSHIRE SPUR.	
"	2/7/17		2 Trench Mortars fired into FEMY WOOD. One from an range on East edge and one on a line of reflext running parallel to the North edge. Firing commenced at 11.0 pm and ceased at 11.10 pm. 46 rounds were fired. No S.O.S. alarm was sounded at 11. 2 pm. Firing pending for shells. No S.O.S. relays to Westward at sector types. Reminder were relieved by a party from Battery types.	
"	3/7/17		We were on fire from 5 Lab on to barricade by a Stokes Mortar.	
"	4/7/17		Stokes fire on Oldham Valley (new) 76 rounds on the corner of FEMY WOOD (Ref. I.53). Very little retaliation. When relieving ammunition carrying. 74 rounds retired from Brigade ammunition Dump.	
"	5/7/17 6/7/17		Operation Order received for the relief of the Brigade by the 195th Brigade. Ammunition order received re the relief. Who should be under R & Mortars. Battery Order issued for the relief. Aug 1. 175th I.M. Battery.	BATTERY ORDERS
"	9/7/17		Provisional Training Programme used to Brigade H.Q. for period 12/16/7/17.	

A.534 Wt. W 4973/M687 750,000 8/16 D.D. & L. Ltd. Forms/C.2118/13

WAR DIARY or INTELLIGENCE SUMMARY

Army Form C. 2118.

Place	Date	Hour	Summary of Events and Information	Remarks and references to Appendices
TRESCAULT (O.14.d.2.3.)	2/9/17		N.C.O. from 173rd R.H.Battery reported at Battery H.Qrs. to take over. The 173rd R.H.A. arrived at H.Qrs. at 11.0pm. Relieving parties proceeded to sections of B.H.A.	
	3/9/17	3.0pm	The Relief was complete by 3.30am.	
	8/9/17	1.30am	The Battery entrained for B.H.S. arriving there 5.0am. Then marched to Camp A16 (BARASTRE). We were rested in the morning. In the afternoon they cleaned equipment, clothing.	
BARASTRE	9/9/17	9.30am	The Battery paraded for march to BIHUCOURT. arrived here at 12.30pm. To was followed on the line spared.	
BIHUCOURT	10/9/17		That Inspection at 10.0am. Remainder of the day spent in general camp fatigues. Men had baths in the afternoon. Orders received for the move of the Brigade to new area. Brigade administrative order issued preparatory move to COURCELLES.	
BIHUCOURT & COURCELLES	11/9/17		Advance party proceeded to COURCELLES. The Battery moved from BIHUCOURT at 10.15am and arrived COURCELLES about noon. Rear party left behind to clear camp and arrived at new quarters 6.0pm.	
		6-7pm	Lecture for Officers at Brigade H.Q. on Discipline.	
COURCELLES	12/9/17		Early morning run from 7.0am to 7.30am. Lecture from 10 to 11. Drivers, Laying out, gun drill & layout training in the afternoon.	

Army Form C. 2118.

WAR DIARY
or
INTELLIGENCE SUMMARY.
(Erase heading not required.)

Place	Date	Hour	Summary of Events and Information	Remarks and references to Appendices
COURCELLES	13/7/19		Training carried on. Orders issued for the inoculation of men who have never inoculated within 12 months. AW	
"	14/7/19		Rose to church in the morning. The Brigadier General inspected the billets at 10 am. Staff holiday in the afternoon. 7 men inoculated at BHQ. AW	
	15/7/19		Ceremonial Drill. Men informed dance in Reading Room. Received training in the afternoon. AW	
	16/7/19		30 men paraded at Town Majors Office for fatigue. AW	
	17/7/19		Training carried on. 7 to 7.30 am Gun Drill. From 9 to 12 noon, Battery Drill. Buying and placement of troops on target. From 2 to 6 pm Gun drill 4-5.30 pm Ceremonial Drill musketry. AW	
	18/7/19		7am to 7.30am Ceremonial Drill. From 9 am to 12 Battery Drill was carried on. Recreational training in the afternoon. AW	
	19/7/19		Men had baths in the morning. Training carried on in the afternoon. Gas Helmet Inspection also carried out by Gas Gas Officer. AW	
	20/7/19		Firing on miniature Range in the morning. AW	
	21/7/19		Squad Drill from 7 am to 7.30 am. Bayonet fighting P.T. Battery Drill and Gun Drill from 9 to 12 noon. AW	

WAR DIARY
INTELLIGENCE SUMMARY.
(Erase heading not required.)

Army Form C. 2118.

Place	Date	Hour	Summary of Events and Information	Remarks and references to Appendices
COURCELLES	22/7/17		Divisional Drill in the morning. Church parade in the afternoon. AWM.	
"	23/7/17		Capt. Wilkinson returned from leave. The daily training programme carried out. No. 295078 Pte. Graham awarded 6 C.B. for a stricke of the plough &. the Gluteal. AWM.	
"	24/7/17		Daily training programme carried out. Firing at Brigade Rifle Range in the afternoon. AWM.	
"	25/7/17		Tactical Scheme carried out in the morning. 50 rounds of ammunition taken out. 44 rounds were fired. AWM.	
"	26/7/17		Training carried on. The miniature range was used in the afternoon. AWM.	
"	27/7/17		Tactical Scheme in conjunction with the 110th MGCoy in the morning from 6 a.m. to 12 noon. At 4:45 p.m. the 2nd Bar of ammunition was fired. AWM.	
"	28/7/17		Training carried on in the morning. Recreation in the afternoon. 2nd Lt Darcy proceeded on leave to U.K. AWM.	
"	29/7/17		No. 295104 Pte Lawson proceeded on leave to U.K. Church parade cancelled owing to bad weather. Divisional Sports in the afternoon. AWM.	
"	30/7/17		Training carried on in the morning. 2nd Lt W. Hunt proceeded on leave to U.K. AWM.	

Army Form C. 2118.

WAR DIARY
INTELLIGENCE SUMMARY.
(Erase heading not required.)

Instructions regarding War Diaries and Intelligence Summaries are contained in F. S. Regs., Part II. and the Staff Manual respectively. Title pages will be prepared in manuscript.

Place	Date	Hour	Summary of Events and Information	Remarks and references to Appendices
COURCELLES	30/9/19		Training carried on. Communication Drill 9½ to 7-30. 9 to 12 noon Msk Inspection reading from Drill 30M.	
	31/9/19			

A.W.Chambers Capt. M/L' R.
for O/C 1st Canadian M.G.Bn.

Orders by Capt. A. J. Hampson OC. 16. MMG. 7/7/17

Orderly officer. Lt. J. Atkinson
Corporal L/Cpl. McHugh

Relief The 175th MGC will relieve the 16th MMG
on the night 7/8 July 17.

Para (1) Relief of gun teams in front line
Gun teams of B. C. & and
Section HQrs when relieved will
proceed in charge of J.C. Bell to Batty HQrs.
The Gun team in F post when
relieved will return direct to Batty HQrs.
All trench stores will be handed over
including screens, camouflage etc.
The following will not be handed over:-
Gun and mounting, cleaning rods,
Spare parts, sup lamps, tommys cookers
these are to be brought back to
Batty HQrs. The base plate only of the
gun is to be left in the emplacement.
Special instructions have been issued
to the gun teams that are to fire prior
to relief. The personnel and handcarts
of the Battery will entrain at Q14 c.2.1.
by midnight and on detraining will
proceed via BUS-BARASTRE road to camp
O16. a. 6. 3. The Battery will be met by guides

on the aforementioned road.

(2) **Day of the 7th July.**
2/Lt H.B. Dewey & 1 O.R. will proceed to BIHUCOURT on the M.G.Co lorry. Time of departure to be notified later. They will act as advanced party and take the unconsumed portion of rations of the 7th 72 days.

(3) **Advanced party No 2.**
2. O.R. will meet the Staff Captain at 10 - am on the 7th inst at crossroads at BARASTRE (O.16.a.6.3).

(4) **Transport.**
2 G.S. Waggons and 1 G.S. limber to be met at B.H.Q. at 10.0 pm. on the 7th inst and guided to Battery Hqrs.
To be loaded as follows.
(a) 1. G.S. Waggon — Kits and packs and necessary stores.
(b) 1. G.S. limber. — 2 guns and 111 Rounds as Mobile Reserve.
(c) 1. G.S. Waggon. 6 guns and stores not required until the unit arrives at its destination.
(a)(b) will travel direct to camp at BARASTRE (O.16.a.6.3). Here the waggon will be unloaded and return.
(c) Will proceed to YPRES railway

siding and be unloaded, and the stores to be loaded in railway trucks, travelling direct to BIHUCOURT. A loading party of 1 NCO and 4 men to proceed with this waggon and travel on the train. 2 days rations will be carried.

(5) On the 8th July. 1 G.S Waggon & 1 G.S. limber will report from D.A.C. 42 Div to carry stores and mobile reserve to BIHUCOURT

(6) July 9th. The Battery will march to BIHUCOURT via RIENCOURT and BAPAUME. The position in column of march will be in rear (no interval) of 176. M.G. Co. Starting point O.15.a.3.4. and to pass this point at 9-29 am on the 9th inst. Watches synchronised

(7) tt from BHQ by telephone at 9.30 pm 8th inst. The G.S Waggon and limber will be in rear of Battery as 1st line transport. On arrival in camp at BIHUCOURT, this transport will return to D.A.C.

(7) March Discipline. A halt of 10 minutes each hour and 5 minutes each ½ hour, and discipline must be strictly enforced, with special attention to the following:—
  (a) Punctuality in reaching starting point

(b) Punctuality in halting and moving off at the time laid down.
(c) Correct side of the road.
(d) No NCO or man to fall out without written authority.
(e) Hand carts must be kept close together.
(f) Precautionary word "Eyes front" to be given before each rest.
(g) When compliments are paid the Senior officer or N.C.O. is to give the precautionary word "Eyes front" and then give the necessary command.
(h) No men are allowed to ride on waggons and only 1 man to march in rear of any waggon. Loading parties will march under the senior N.C.O. as a party.

Rations

When drawn	Place	For consumption	Transport
July 8th and	YPRES	9th July	Handcarts
— — from	—	10th —	430. A.S.C.
— 10th	G.D.a. Cross roads BEAUCOURT	11th —	M.G.C.

6/7/17.

Signed L. J. Hampson
O.C. A.h. S.t. M.R.

Army Form C. 2118.

WAR DIARY
or
INTELLIGENCE SUMMARY.
(*Erase heading not required.*)

126th Light Trench Mortar Battery

Volume VI

August 1st 1917 to August 31st 1917

Army Form C. 2118.

WAR DIARY
or
INTELLIGENCE SUMMARY.
(Erase heading not required.)

Instructions regarding War Diaries and Intelligence
Summaries are contained in F. S. Regs., Part II.
and the Staff Manual respectively. Title pages
will be prepared in manuscript.

Place	Date	Hour	Summary of Events and Information	Remarks and references to Appendices
COURCELLES	1/9/17		Daily training programme carried out. Recreational training in the afternoon. Training programme for week ending 10th July sent to Bde. ADM. War Diary for the month of July sent to Bde. ADM.	
"	2/9/17		Stokes Guns & Lewis Guns taken to training area. Emplacements dug in preparation for the Brigade scheme. ADM	
"	3/9/17		The Battery paraded at 6 a.m. and marched to training area to take part in Brigade scheme. Guns in position by 8 a.m. C.O.s Conference at H.Q. at 5.30 p.m. Returned from scheme at 12.30 p.m. ADM.	
"	4/9/17		Early morning parade. Musketry Trench training in the morning. Half holiday in the afternoon. Paid the men of the Battery. ADM.	
"	5/9/17		Church Parade for the Brigade at 9 men in orchard near 15 West fence of Hqrs. The presentation of ribbons by the Divisional Commander postponed. Brigade Sports postponed until further notice. ADM	

WAR DIARY
INTELLIGENCE SUMMARY.

Army Form C. 2118.

Place	Date	Hour	Summary of Events and Information	Remarks and references to Appendices
COURCELLES	6/9/17		Daily training programme carried out consisting of Personal Drill. Bayonet Fighting. Section Drill. Lewis Gun Drill. Buzzing. Replacements. JDA	
	7/9/17		C.O. Inspection in the morning. Parade at noon for the Brigade scheme. JDA	
	8/9/17		Battery arrived back from the scheme at 5.30 a.m. Men rested in the morning. Cleaned ammunition in the afternoon. Training programme for next week drawn up & sent to R.H.Q. JDA	
	9/9/17		Training for the day consisted of squad drill, lecture on employment of Lewis Gun in Village & Wood fighting. Night scheme with dummy enemy 9.10pm to 11.20 pm. Lt. Meakin to proceed to Tortuere to attend C.O. course at the Divisional Bombing School. JDA	
	10/9/17		Called the "Ruta Jour" on previous night. Men kept in the afternoon. JDA	

WAR DIARY
INTELLIGENCE SUMMARY

Army Form C. 2118.

Place	Date	Hour	Summary of Events and Information	Remarks and references to Appendices
CORCELLES	1/8/17		Section in scheme in conjunction with 1/9 Manchester Regt and 1 section in conjunction with 1/10 Manchester Regt. Brigade Sports in the afternoon.	
	5/8/17		At C of E church parade (several recalls) owing to wet weather. 10 men of the Battery (mounted) with other men for the interment of remains by the Major Funeral.	
	7/8/17		Section on scheme in conjunction with 1/4 East Lanc Regt in a trench attack. Remainder carried on with the Daily Training Programme. 2nd/Lt the men of the Battery.	
	10/8/17		On the Miniature Range in the morning. In the afternoon the finding of Stokes guns in front to trench attack.	
	11/8/17		Training for the day: Battery drill with trumpet Gas Mask Bayonet fighting, Recreational Training. 10 395066 Pte Francis admitted to Hospital.	

Army Form C. 2118.

WAR DIARY
INTELLIGENCE SUMMARY.
(Erase heading not required.)

Place	Date	Hour	Summary of Events and Information	Remarks and references to Appendices
COURCELLES	16/9/17		The Battery paraded for Bath at 8.0am. Lecture at 10.0am on "Trench to Trench Attack" General Drill 11 to 12. 3 Men proceeded by train to aerodrome at V Corps School at 1-30pm.	
	17/9/17		Battery paraded at 9.0am marched to trenches at M.D. 4.B. Battery drilling with live firing carried out.	
	18/9/17		Morning parade consisted of General Drill Supply emplacement, Bayonet Fighting. Bayonet stops in the afternoon. Remainder of the battery proceeded by lorry to the show ground returned for an early dinner by march route.	
	19/9/17		Church parade in the morning. Enemy Stokes shells the remainder of the morning. Operation & Ammunition Orders received for the move to next area.	
	20/9/17		Transport (1 lorry) arrived at 9.0am to take stores to new area. 1 N.C.O. & 7 men proceeded in charge of same. Cpl Dobson reported to Capt Lillie at H.Q. to proceed in advance & take over billets. Cpl Stockton reported at R.T.O. Office at 1. 0pm & along with representatives	

A.5834 Wt. W.4973/M687 750,000 8/16 D.D. & L. Ltd. Forms/C.2118/13.

Army Form C. 2118.

WAR DIARY
or
INTELLIGENCE SUMMARY.

(Erase heading not required.)

Instructions regarding War Diaries and Intelligence Summaries are contained in F. S. Regs., Part II. and the Staff Manual respectively. Title pages will be prepared in manuscript.

Place	Date	Hour	Summary of Events and Information	Remarks and references to Appendices
COURCELLES	18/8/17		Officers went on the Brigade grounds in advance to the final instructions.	
COURCELLES	19/8/17		The Battery paraded at 9:15 a.m. for the march to BERTRANCOURT. Starting point at R.H.Q. at 9:30 a.m. Arrived BERTRANCOURT 2.30 p.m. No man fell out on the line of march.	Battery Orders No. 17
BERTRANCOURT				
"	20/8/17		Departed from BERTRANCOURT at 11 a.m. marched to BEAUCOURT-SUR-ANCRE. Entrained here at 10.30. Train moved away at 11 p.m. Arrived at detraining station at about midnight. Unloaded trucks & marched to TRAPPESTES and billetted there.	Battery Orders No. 17
TRAPPESTES	21/8/17		Men rested during the day.	
"	22/8/17		Kit Inspection General Court Inturned Received Maps of New Area	
"	23/8/17		Training carried on in the morning.	
"	24/8/17		Church Parade in Camp of 1/16 4 1/16 Mdx Regt. Ceremonial Drill	
"	25/8/17		Daily training programme consisted of Gun Drill Anyard Fighting, Battery Drill, Route March.	

WAR DIARY or INTELLIGENCE SUMMARY.

Army Form C. 2118.

Place	Date	Hour	Summary of Events and Information	Remarks and references to Appendices
TRAPPISTES	28/9/17		Daily training programme carried out. Preparatory Warning Order received for a move to YPRES. Operation of Municipal Water Supplies received for the move. JOHR	
"	29/9/17		Training carried out in the morning. Training cancelled for the afternoon. Men had the use of baths at MAPOV from 10p.m. to 5.30p.m. Addendum 1, 2, +3 to administrative Instruction received. Advance party of 1 Off. 3 O.R. proceeded by lorry to YPRES to take over billets Pharmacie.	Battery Order No 179
"	30/9/17 YPRES		The Battery paraded at 10-0 a.m. for the march to YPRES. One Officer & 3 O.R. who received (?) as road party. The Battery arrived at YPRES SOUTH at 4.15 p.m. No men fell out on the line of march. JOHR	
"	30/9/17		General Camp Fatigues during the day. 2 men rejoined the Battery from leave. JOHR	

J.H. Hampson Capt
Burg R.H.B

WAR DIARY
or
INTELLIGENCE SUMMARY.

Army Form C. 2118.

Confidential

126th Light Trench Mortar Battery.

Volume VII.

From Sept 1st 1917 to Sept 30th 1917.

Army Form C. 2118.

WAR DIARY
or
INTELLIGENCE SUMMARY.
(Erase heading not required.)

Instructions regarding War Diaries and Intelligence Summaries are contained in F. S. Regs., Part II. and the Staff Manual respectively. Title pages will be prepared in manuscript.

Place	Date	Hour	Summary of Events and Information	Remarks and references to Appendices
YPRES	1/9/17		Go Kit and Drill and Inspection. Several camp fatigues. 2 OR's reported to Factory from leave. No 795085 76 Meerken N. proceeded (left) (paid). No 95091 Hipf. Brown promoted Cpl. JM	
"	2/9/17		No.1 Sub section under the Lieutenant proceeded to RAILWAY WOOD in support. Remainder of the Battery paraded at 9.30 am for camp fatigues. No 7509/ Pte Hylden [illegible] at 9 pm & would evacuated to Ulster on aspect for wounds received at the front and thought to be attempt of the Battery. He 9786 Hw baker on the strength of the Bay & lasted on allotment. JM	BATTERY OPERATION ORDER No 1
"	3/9/17		9.30 am Bayonet Fighting. Battery Drill and Training of newly attached reinforcement from Ymuiden. JM	
"	4/9/17		No. 2 sub section, under the Lieutenant, proceeded to Lichentyr in Railway Wood to relieve No. 1 sub section under Lt [illegible]. Remainder paraded at 9.30 am for Drill & Bayonet Fighting. JM	Battery Operation Order No 2
"	5/9/17		The men paraded at 9.30am for work on dug out & shelters. Lt Statendam proceeded to UK on leave. JM	
"	6/9/17		No 3 sub section under Col Baely proceeded to declare lines and relieved No 2 sub section. Remainder continued work on shelters & dug outs. JM	Battery Op. Order No 3
"	7/9/17		Work continued on dug outs & shelters. JM	

WAR DIARY
or
INTELLIGENCE SUMMARY.

(Erase heading not required.)

Army Form C. 2118.

Place	Date	Hour	Summary of Events and Information	Remarks and references to Appendices
YPRES	9/9/17		No 4 Sub section under 2/Lt Ball proceeded to Section Hqrs and relieved No 3 Sub section under 2/Lt Ainsworth. Remainder of the Battery carried out work on shelters. B/M	Battery Operation Order No. 4
	9/9/17		Work continued on dug out shelters. In accordance with S.R.O 2348 2/Lt Williams and 2/Lt McSweeny are struck off the strength of the Battery (and the Section) No. 15.38/702 of 8/9. DM	
	10/9/17		No. 1 Sub section under 2/Lt Keersley proceeded to Section Hqrs on Railway Wood and relieved No. 2 Sub section. Remainder working on dug outs. No 2005/6 Bombdr McDonough was admitted to hospital, sick reported for duty and is taken on the arrived strength of the Battery. DM/M	Copy of Operation Order No. 5
	11/9/17		The Battery paraded at 9 am for fatigues. No 3103.Sr H Moss returned to Field Amb. (sick) DM	
	12/9/17		No 2 Sub section under 2/Lt Ainsworth proceeded at 5.15 am forward to Section Hqrs and relieved No1 Sub section under 2/Lt Beale. DM/M	Battery Operation Order No. 6
	13/9/17		No 2025/8 Sr Hampson W/S Gunn Repl and 1/6 M/S Kingman Repl Joined the Battery from leave. M	
	14/9/17		No 7 sub section under 2/Lt Ball proceeded Section Hqrs and relieved 1/6 5 Jas returned to Sector under 2/Lt Ainsworth. DM/M	Military Oper. Orders No 7

WAR DIARY / INTELLIGENCE SUMMARY

Army Form C. 2118.

Place	Date	Hour	Summary of Events and Information	Remarks and references to Appendices
YPRES	15/9/17		Several fatigue parties detailed to clear rations up the line. 2nd Lieut. reported to Brigade Hqrs for instructions. 2nd Lieut York leaves H.Q. at 9 p.m. (one left) and 2nd Lieut. Ainsworth & 2nd Lieut taken on the establishment of the Battery from 14/9/17 vice 2nd Lieut Aland and 2nd Lieut Doury, struck off strength (Authy 1/6 2nd Bde.) DOM	
	16/9/17		Operation Order and Administration Order received for the relief of 2/7/9 By the Battery. Orders issued for the move. No 3 Inspection returned from Leave. Major Hardey-Wood at 7.0 pm. Incoming march took over. The Battery left Ypres at 1130 pm and marched to BEDOUIN CAMP arriving there soon after 10 pm.	Battery Office Order No 8
BEDOUIN CAMP (RANDHOEK)	17/9/17		1 NCO and men reported to Battery from Corps Small Arms Repair Shop left tomorrow hot Camps for orders. DOM The greater part of the Maelos (10 small provided) fitted during the day.	
	18/9/17		Orders received for the move to new Area. Major Inglehurst, Gunner Brice and Gun cleaning during the morning. DOM	Battery Operation Order No 9

WAR DIARY
of
INTELLIGENCE SUMMARY.

Army Form C. 2118.

Place	Date	Hour	Summary of Events and Information	Remarks and references to Appendices
WINNEZEELE	19/9/17		Battery paraded at 5. am and Marched to WINNEZEELE. Advanced party proceded to WINNEZEELE at 3. am. Battery arrived at 10-30 am. No men fell out on the line of march. Training programme sent to Brigade.	
	20/9/17		Training carried on for 2 hours. Remainder of the day spent in cleaning up. Warning Order received for the move to WORMHOUDT. Operation and Administrative orders issued for the move.	Battery Orders No 10
WORMHOUDT	21/9/17		The Battery paraded at 10 am for the march to WORMHOUDT. Arrived here at 1-30 pm. Operation and Movement orders Received for the move to TETEGHEM.	Battery Orders No 11
TETEGHEM	22/9/17		The Advance Party left for TETEGHEM at 5. am. The Battery paraded at 9. am and marched to TETEGHEM. No men fell out on the line of march. Operation and Movement Order received for the move to LA PANNE. Advance party left at 11-30 pm	Battery Orders No 12
LA PANNE	23/9/17		Battery paraded at 7 am for the march to LA PANNE. Arrived there 1-30pm. Operation order and Administrative orders issued for the move to COXYDE BAINS.	Battery Orders No 13

Army Form C. 2118.

WAR DIARY
or
INTELLIGENCE SUMMARY.
(Erase heading not required.)

Instructions regarding War Diaries and Intelligence
Summaries are contained in F. S. Regs., Part II.
and the Staff Manual respectively. Title pages
will be prepared in manuscript.

Place	Date	Hour	Summary of Events and Information	Remarks and references to Appendices
OXYDE BAINS	24/9/17		The Battery paraded at 8.15am and marched to OXYDE BAINS. Arrived there at 11am and took over from 198 S.T.M. Battery.	
	25/9/17		The Battery paraded at 9am for fatigues. Remainder of the day fatigues except officers.	
	26/9/17		Daily training programme carried out.	
	27/9/17		Training carried on. Men took the use of Personnel tested from 11am to 12 noon. 3 men from Reinforcement Camp joined the Battery and taken on attached strength.	
	28/9/17		Daily training programme carried out. No. 3701 Gr. Marlin rejoined the Battery from 5th Army Rest Camp.	
	29/9/17		Training carried on. Lt. Paterson 9th M. Division att'd 176 S.T.M.C. reverted 2nd Ambulance. To Hosp. The Gerry & East Lancs. left, struck off the attached strength of this unit.	
	2/10/17		Kit parade at 11am in tent district. Recreational training in the afternoon. Nos 15079 Cpl Boulton proceeded to the first four day course at the Div. Gas School.	

Signed

O.C. 176 S.T.M. Battery

Army Form C. 2118.

WAR DIARY
or
INTELLIGENCE SUMMARY.
(Erase heading not required.)

126th Light Trench Mortar Battery

Volume VIII.

From Oct 1st 1917 to Oct 31st 1917.

Army Form C. 2118.

WAR DIARY
or
INTELLIGENCE SUMMARY.
(Erase heading not required.)

Place	Date	Hour	Summary of Events and Information	Remarks and references to Appendices
Coxyde Bains	1/10/17		Daily training programme carried out. Lt. E. Bull rejoined the Battery from leave.	
	2/10/17		Daily training programme carried out.	
	3/10/17		Daily training programme carried out.	
	4/10/17		Firm's camp fatigues done at day. Warning orders received for the move of the Brigade to the NIEUPORT sector. Lieut. H. Rogers & 26 O.R. proceed to there to act as instructors in Lewis Mortars.	
	5/10/17		Lt. Col. Gill Foster rejoined the Battery from Divl. Gas Course. Operation and miscellaneous orders received for the relief of the Brigade by the 126th Brigade. Coast Defence duties and the relief of the Battery by the 126th Brigade. Orders issued for the relief of the 146th Bn F.A. by the 126th 120th R.	Battery Orders No. 14

Army Form C. 2118.

WAR DIARY
or
INTELLIGENCE SUMMARY.
(Erase heading not required.)

Instructions regarding War Diaries and Intelligence Summaries are contained in F. S. Regs., Part II. and the Staff Manual respectively. Title pages will be prepared in manuscript.

Place	Date	Hour	Summary of Events and Information	Remarks and references to Appendices
NIEUPORT	6/10/17		The Battery paraded at 9.30 a.m. and marched to NIEUPORT, and took over from the 19th T.M.B.:1	
"	7/10/17		Guns taken over are the liner Battery of 6 Guns located at the SARDINERIE. Relief completed at 5.0 p.m. No casualties. JMW	
			Hostile Artillery was very active on back areas during the night. The SARDINERIE apparently were heavily shelled during the period. It was 6 hrs for the Highlanders attached to the Battery for instruction for 3 days. JMW	
"	8/10/17		Hostile artillery activity great on the forward area. The SARDINERIE was shelled with different calibres from 9.30 pm to 10.30 pm. JMW	
"	9/10/17		A new Defence emplacement has been started at N.31. K.3. L. Hostile artillery fairly quiet. Work carried on re-improving emplacements, retaining accommodation. JMW	
"	10/10/17		All other Guns were registered on their S.O.S. lines and alterations made where necessary. JMW	

A5834 Wt.W4973/M687 750,000 8/16 D. D. & L. Ltd. Forms/C.2118/13.

Army Form C. 2118.

WAR DIARY
or
INTELLIGENCE SUMMARY.
(Erase heading not required.)

Place	Date	Hour	Summary of Events and Information	Remarks and references to Appendices
NIEUPORT	10/10/17		Hostile artillery active during the night on back areas. New defensive emplacement at N.3.d.3.4. nearly completed. Dug out also partly completed. A new defensive gun position at M.30.a.45.55. commenced. MGW	
	1/10/17		The emplacement at N.3.d.3.4. completed. MM. At M.30 a.45.55 nearly completed. MM. New defensive emplacement. A few 77 m.m. shells fell near new defensive position M.30.d.60.83 during the day. Work commenced on dug out for above position. Lt. W.J. Redston 1/4 York. Regts. att'd 1/4 East Lancs Regt. reported for duty to this unit and taken on attached strength. MGW	
	1/10/17	2:30 to 4:30 pm	The CHURCH (NIEUPORT) apparently were heavily shelled by 4.2" from Emplacement at M.30 a.45.55. was completed. Ammunition store commenced for this emplacement. No. 795109 Cpl. Dowsley promoted Sergt. (date) 1/9/17. B. completed to relieve dispatch. MGW	

WAR DIARY
or
INTELLIGENCE SUMMARY.
(Erase heading not required.)

Army Form C. 2118.

Place	Date	Hour	Summary of Events and Information	Remarks and references to Appendices
NIEUPORT	12/10/17		Hostile artillery very quiet. Dug out for Rations at N 3 f 3.4 and N 30 a 45.55 nearly completed. Ammunition store at N 30 a 45.55 nearly completed. OMN	
	13/10/17		Hostile artillery fairly quiet. Ammunition recess completed. Work on general improvement of emplacements going on. H.E. Ball relieved Lt. Ainsworth at the H.qrs. Lt. Ainsworth on relief proceeded to rear H.qrs. JMN	
	14/10/17		Hostile artillery slightly active. Ammunition recess completed. General improvement of emplacement and general ammunition. JMN	
	15/10/17		Lt. Ainsworth proceeded to England on 10 days leave. JMN No. 45092 Cpl Procter proceeded to Hospital Wimereux for examination of eyes. Hostile artillery normal. JMN	
	16/10/17		Improvements & Mereur Bastion commenced. JMN	

WAR DIARY
or
INTELLIGENCE SUMMARY.

Place	Date	Hour	Summary of Events and Information	Remarks and references to Appendices
NIEUPORT	17/10/17		Hostile artillery quiet on forward area. Enemy offensive position at M20. a. 6.75 occupied. Work on improvement of dug outs carried out. Orders received for the relief of our teams.	Battery Orders No 15.
	18/10/17		No. 38710 the Lieut attached 2nd Auk 16/10/17. Hostile artillery active during the night on NIEUPORT. Men worked ordinary connection in offensive defence positions.	
	19/10/17		Hostile activity (artillery) much above normal. The right section front system of trenches was rather heavily shelled. The defensive gun emplacement ammunition store at N.31. b.4.6. were destroyed. No ex/losion occurred. Work started on enlarging the gun & ammunition at N.31. b.25. & N.31. b.4.6.	

WAR DIARY or INTELLIGENCE SUMMARY

Army Form C. 2118.

Place	Date	Hour	Summary of Events and Information	Remarks and references to Appendices
NIEUPORT	25/9/17		Hostile artillery active during the night. A number of gas shells were fired into NIEUPORT. Work carried on and salvaging ammunition at N.31.b.3.5. N.31.b.1.6. the offensive position of ½ gun (N.30.a.95.95.) complete. AJM	
	26/9/17		Fairly quiet day. Work carried on in general cleaning up. Hostile artillery active at night on no normal target in NIEUPORT. AJM	
	27/9/17		NIEUPORT. After some few shells dropped near the Church it appeared to (QUEEN ELIZABETH BRIDGE). Enemy aeroplane were fairly active over our lines. 1 N.C.O. intended the S.E. course at the Kenflo School. AJM	
	28/9/17		General activity much below normal. AJM	
	29/9/17		Hostile artillery fairly active. The BARDINERIE & enemy were shelled from 2.0 to 3 p.m. by the MH. The sundries during the night. Work carried on in cleaning up. AJM	

WAR DIARY
or
INTELLIGENCE SUMMARY.
(Erase heading not required.)

Army Form C. 2118.

Place	Date	Hour	Summary of Events and Information	Remarks and references to Appendices
NIEUPORT	24/9/17		Hostile artillery fire normal. NASTY TRENCH was heavily shelled during the night. Parapet was partly damaged. 223 rounds 3" Stokes shell were carried up to the right sector to replace ammunition which had been damaged. Salvaged ammunition was brought back. 30/N	
	26/9/17		Hostile activity below normal. Work carried on chiefly ammunition. 30/N	Battn. Orders No. 16.
	27/9/17		Hostile artillery very active in the morning on our forward area in St GEORGES SECTOR. Fairly busy for relief of gun teams. No 275155 Sergt Lewis H of Manchester Reg't act'd 126 Lt M.B. proceeded to Maresco for duty as an instructor in Stokes Mortars. The MFC212 accompanied him. Both R.G. MM'S A.F. 107 and E. 29/9/17. 30/N	
	28/9/17		Hostile artillery very quiet. A few gas shells were dropped in NIEUPORT in the afternoon leading to ROBERT + QUEEN ELIZABETH BRIDGE. Hostile Aeroplane active during the morning. W.E. Price 1/n Lieut. Hants Reg't attach'd 15th East Lanc Reg't is taken on the total strength of the 126 Lt M Battery from 29/9/17 (auth. A.A. MH A/09/19 of 9/11)	

WAR DIARY or INTELLIGENCE SUMMARY

Army Form C. 2118.

Place	Date	Hour	Summary of Events and Information	Remarks and references to Appendices
NIEUPORT	28/10/17		2/Lt Winworth 16th Manchester Regt is taken on the establishment of the 126th L.T.M. Battery from 11/10/17. (Auth. H.Q. I.M.A. A/109/10/01.) 2/Lt J. Gordon If. of pdr. Heavy Regt. and 1st East Lancs Regt is taken on the establishment of the 126th L.T.M. Battery from 14/10/17. (Auth. No. S.M. A/109/10/01) 2/Lt E. Rues 5/7th Manchester (France) being Rank of whilst 2nd Lieut. No 375155. Sergt. Lewis 1/10 Manchester Regt having proceeded to America East as instructor on Stokes Mortars, is struck off the strength of this Battery. No 78056 Cpl. McHugh 1/6 Manchester Regt. reverts to reverts rank (from Sgt.) dated 7/10/17. Also No 75153 Sgt Lewis to remain. No 29035 Acpl Meakin 1/6 Manchester Regt and 1/26 T.T.M B to be Corporal dated 28/9/17, to complete establishment.	
	29/10/17		Hostile artillery lots normal. E.A. were fairly active during the morning.	

WAR DIARY
or
INTELLIGENCE SUMMARY.
(Erase heading not required.)

Army Form C. 2118.

Place	Date	Hour	Summary of Events and Information	Remarks and references to Appendices
NIEUPORT	20/10/17		Hostile artillery fairly active. The forward gun position at N 30 a.8.7. was hit this accumulation destroyed. E.A. were active over our lines during the morning. Lt. J. Ainsworth 11th Manchesters left at 11.16 to shift ground the Battery from base.	
"	21/10/17		Hostile artillery klier normal. Both carried on exploding scattered ammunition at N 30 a.8.7. Lt. E. O. Morris 11th Manchester Regt joined the Battery for duty.	

21/10/17

R.P. Humphrey Capt
O.C. A.30 Bomb.

Confidential

Army Form C. 2118.

WAR DIARY
INTELLIGENCE SUMMARY.
(Erase heading not required.)

126th Light Trench Mortar Battery.

Volume IX.

From Nov 1st 1917 to Nov 30th 1917

Army Form C. 2118.

WAR DIARY
or
INTELLIGENCE SUMMARY.
(Erase heading not required.)

Instructions regarding War Diaries and Intelligence Summaries are contained in F. S. Regs., Part II. and the Staff Manual respectively. Title pages will be prepared in manuscript.

Place	Date	Hour	Summary of Events and Information	Remarks and references to Appendices
NIEUPORT	1/11/17		Hostile Artillery fairly active. He attacked to ALBERT and ELIZABETH Bridges bore shelled at intervals through the night. The Minnine position at N.75.a.00.15 was pandbagged and repaired. War Diary for the month of Oct sent to B.H.Q. RB/	
"	2/11/17		Hostile Artillery active on forward areas. The emplacement at N.20.a.6.9½ was blown up and the gun buried. 1. O.R. reported to the Battery for duty to replace casualty. R/	
"	3/11/17		Fairly quiet day. Work carried on with repairing damaged gun pits. 1. O.R. reported for duty to the Battery to replace casualty. R/	
"	4/11/17		Hostile Artillery very active during the day on NIEUPORT and back areas. E.A. were active between 3. a.m. & 10.a.m. flying very low over our lines and NIEUPORT. RB/	
"	5/11/17		The SARDINERIE and tracks in front of our lines shelled at intervals	

A5834 Wt. W4973/M687 750,000 8/16 D. D. & L. Ltd. Forms/C.2118/13.

Army Form C. 2118.

WAR DIARY
or
INTELLIGENCE SUMMARY.
(Erase heading not required.)

Instructions regarding War Diaries and Intelligence Summaries are contained in F. S. Regs., Part II. and the Staff Manual respectively. Title pages will be prepared in manuscript.

Place	Date	Hour	Summary of Events and Information	Remarks and references to Appendices
NIEUPORT	6/11/17		Work carried on improving gun emplacements. EB	
"	7/11/17		Hostile activity below normal. Fairly quiet day. EB	
"	8/11/17		Hostile activity normal. Nothing to report. EB	
"	9/11/17		Hostile artillery fairly active. Heavy shelling of NIEUPORT. 1st 2 guns at N.N.6-N.5. 18th was withdrawn into rest at the Casserne & O.R. taken on the strength of the Battery to complete establishment. EB	
"	9/11/17		Hostile activity normal. Nothing to report. EB	
"	10/11/17		Hostile artillery active on left Batt. front and back areas. EB	
"	11/11/17		Nieuport was shelled rather heavily through the day. 1 O.R. wounded and struck off the strength of the Battery. W. Macaulay 2/Lt. Macaulay No. 29302 A/Bombr. W. Macaulay left. attached 126 Light T.M. Battery	

A.5834 Wt. W4973/M687 750,000 8/16 D. D. & L. Ltd. Forms/C.2118/13.

Army Form C. 2118.

WAR DIARY
or
INTELLIGENCE SUMMARY.
(Erase heading not required.)

Instructions regarding War Diaries and Intelligence Summaries are contained in F. S. Regs., Part II and the Staff Manual respectively. Title pages will be prepared in manuscript.

Place	Date	Hour	Summary of Events and Information	Remarks and references to Appendices
NIEUPORT			awarded the Military Medal. EBJ	
"	12/11/17		Nieuport was again shelled frequently through the day. 2nd Lt. E.O. Morris 1/10th Manchester left and is to proceed on 14 days leave to England. EBJ	
"	13/11/17		Hostile Artillery above normal shelling of NIEUPORT. 1 O.R. rejoined the Battery from leave. EBJ	
"	14/11/17		General shelling of NIEUPORT. E.A. were very active during the day. EBJ	
"	15/11/17		Hostile Artillery normal. The 1/5th Nature of Stokes ammunition returned to railhead. 176 2/Lt. Pte Warning order received. EBJ	
"	16/11/17		Nieuport CHURCH heavily shelled from 6.30am to 10am, otherwise shelling of Nieuport was lighter than on previous days. EBJ	

Army Form C. 2118.

WAR DIARY
or
INTELLIGENCE SUMMARY.
(Erase heading not required.)

Place	Date	Hour	Summary of Events and Information	Remarks and references to Appendices
NIEUPORT			E.A. were active through the day. Operation orders received for the relief of the Brigade by a Brigade of the 17th French Division. Battery orders issued for the withdrawal of the Battery from the line owing to no unit relieving the Battery E.B/	BATTERY ORDERS No. 18
	19/11/17		Bombardment in the line released by two of the French Division. E.B/	
	19/11/17		The Battery was withdrawn from the line at dusk this was completed without casualties. On completion of the withdrawal the Battery moved & billetted at OOST DUNKERKE.	Battery Orders ref No. 19
			Orders issued for the move of the Battery to WORMHOUDT & thence to ADINKERKE. E.B/	
OOST-DUNKERKE and WORMHOUDT.	19/11/17		The Battery paraded at 6.noon for the march to ADINKERKE. Entrained at ADINKERKE for BRUGES. Debarged at BRUGES and marched to WORMHOUDT, arriving there at 6. p.m. Capt J. Thompson 1/10 th Manchester Regt acted as Town Marshal at Bruges) on 14 days leave. E.B/	

Army Form C. 2118.

WAR DIARY
or
INTELLIGENCE SUMMARY.
(Erase heading not required.)

Place	Date	Hour	Summary of Events and Information	Remarks and references to Appendices
WORMHOUDT	19/11/17		Orders issued for the march to WORMHOUDT "B" area. RB/	Battery Orders No 19.
"	20/11/17		The Battery paraded at 10.30 a.m. and marched to WORMHOUDT "B" area. Operation orders issued for the move to STAPLE area. Battery Orders issued for the move of the Battery to STAPLE area. RB/	Battery Orders No 20
STAPLE area	21/11/17		The Battery paraded at 8.30 a.m. and marched to STAPLE area. Operation and Administrative orders issued for the move to AIRE area. Battery Orders issued for the march to WARNE. RB/	Battery Orders No 21
WARNE	22/11/17		The Battery paraded at 8.15 a.m. and marched to WARNE. Arrived at WARNE 1.0 p.m. No men fell out on the line of march. RB/	
"	23/11/17		General fatigues and cleaning up. RB/	
"	24/11/17		Rifle inspection. Cleaning guns and making limbers etc. Warning order received for the move of the Brigade and relief of the 2nd Division by the 12th Div. RB/	

WAR DIARY
or
INTELLIGENCE SUMMARY.

(Erase heading not required.)

Army Form C. 2118.

Place	Date	Hour	Summary of Events and Information	Remarks and references to Appendices
WARNE	25/11/17		Voluntary Church Parade. Recreational training in the afternoon. EB/	
	26/11/17		Operation and Administrative Orders received for the move of the Brigade to Burgundy Reserve. Battery Orders issued for the move to AIRE 'C' area. EB/	Battery Orders No 22
MOLINGHEM	27/11/17		Battery paraded at 9.30 a.m. and marched to MOLINGHAM and took over billets. Orders received for the move to BETHUNE area. EB/	Administrative & Battery Orders No 23
BETHUNE	28/11/17		Battery paraded at 8.30 a.m. for the march to BETHUNE area. Arrived BETHUNE 2.30 p.m. and took over billets. EB/	
	29/11/17		The Battery paraded at 9 a.m. by inspection Department. Lecture in the afternoon on Musical Reception. EB/	
	30/11/17		Battery paraded at 9 a.m. for rifle inspection. Cleaning guns and inspection of same. EB/ Bath in the afternoon.	E Bull Lieut R.F.A. O.C. 126 S. Battery

WAR DIARY
or
INTELLIGENCE SUMMARY.

Army Form C. 2118.

126th Light Trench Mortar Battery.

Volume X

From 1st Decr. 1917. to 31st Decr. 1917.

Army Form C. 2118.

WAR DIARY
or
INTELLIGENCE SUMMARY.
(Erase heading not required.)

Place	Date	Hour	Summary of Events and Information	Remarks and references to Appendices
BETHUNE	1/7/17		War Diary for the month of Nov. kept to Brigade HQ. Training Programme carried out for the day, consisting of Gun Drill, laying on target, and Physical Drill. Recreational training in the afternoon. Lt. & C. Morris & 4 other Ranks att'd 156 L.T.M.B. rejoined the Battery from Leave. MM	
"	2/7/17		Training for the day consisted of recreational training. Church parade in the morning. MM	
"	3/7/17		Inspection of Gun Helmets & Gas Drill. Gun Drill & run Drill. 1 O.R. proceeded to the Brigade School for Physical & Bayonet fighting Course. 1 O.R. rejoined from leave. MM	
"	4/7/17		Route March in the morning. Recreational training in the afternoon. MM	
"	5/7/17		Training in the morning consisted of Physical & Bayonet fighting, rapid loading on targets. B.C. reparation APPlelonk late in the afternoon by the Div. Gas Officer. MM	
"	6/7/17		Squad Drill, with Arms, Musketry, Gun Drill. Recreational training in the afternoon.	

WAR DIARY or INTELLIGENCE SUMMARY.

Army Form C. 2118.

Place	Date	Hour	Summary of Events and Information	Remarks and references to Appendices
BETHUINE	6/4/17		Capt W. Thompson 1/10 M'dex Regt. att'd 176 S.T.M.Battery beyond the Battery from leave. 1.O.R. evacuated to C.C.S. Struck off the strength of the unit. M.N.	
"	7/4/17		Report fighting Battery Drill & Musketry. General fatigues in the afternoon. Battery paid out. M.N.	
"	8/4/17		Administrative Orders issued for the move of the Brigade to relieve 175 S.T. Brigade. Training programme for the day consisted of Shrapnel Drill, Squad Drill & Battery Drill. M.N.	
"	9/4/17		Divine service in the morning. Lecture given to the Battery on "Allways Fuze". Battery Orders issued for the relief of the 1/XI S.T.M.Battery by 176 T.M.Battery. M.N.	BATTERY ORDERS No 23
"	10/4/17		Battery paraded at 7:45 a.m. and marched to Le PREOL, and took over Wagons from 1/XI S.T.M.B. Relief completed by 1-20 p.m. without casualties. M.N.	
Le PREOL	11/4/17		Hostile Artillery fairly quiet except for a heavy bombardment on our left between 11 a.m. and 2 a.m. 20 rounds Stokes ammunition were fired on BRICKBAT ALLEY. 10 rounds were fired on the L.O.L. line	

Army Form C. 2118.

WAR DIARY
or
INTELLIGENCE SUMMARY.
(Erase heading not required.)

Place	Date	Hour	Summary of Events and Information	Remarks and references to Appendices
LE PREOL	17/17/17		at F16.a.9.8. and BILL EXTENSION in retaliation to the enemy's short bombardment of our lines on the Left Battalion front. JMcD.	
			116 rounds were fired at periods during the day & night. The following targets were engaged :- FRANKS KEEP, RYAN KEEP, BRICKBAT ALLEY, SPOTTED DOG ALLEY and ENEMY BRICKSTACKS. Enemy did not retaliate during the night to our bursts of fire.	
			A new emplacement was made also the gun moved and registered at A. 21. d. 18. 75. Work carried out not dug out for T&Dguns at A15. b. 70. 65.	
			1. O.R. admitted to Field Amb. suffering from the effects of gas. MN.	
	18/17/17		Enemy TM's were fairly quiet during the day but active during the night. 51 rounds were fired during the day & night on the following targets :- S. End of BRICKBAT ALLEY, Vicinity of BRICKSTACKS, RYANS KEEP and EMBANKMENT REDOUBT.	
			1. O.R. proceed to the 8th Div. Gas Course at ESSARS. JMcD.	

Army Form C. 2118.

WAR DIARY
or
INTELLIGENCE SUMMARY.
(Erase heading not required.)

Place	Date	Hour	Summary of Events and Information	Remarks and references to Appendices
Le PREOL	14/1/17		Enemy showed very little activity during day & night. Stokes Mortars fired 166 rounds on the following targets: SPOTTED DOG ALLEY, H.L. IM BRICKSTACKS, BILL EXTENSION, BRICKBAT ALLEY, FRANKS KEEP, RYAN'S KEEP, and various trench junctions. The only time the enemy seriously retaliated was on the 3 occasions when BILL EXTENSION was fired on. 3 O.R. proceeded on leave (10 days) to England. MW	
	15/1/17		106 rounds Stokes Mortars were fired during the day & night, the following targets were engaged: BRICKBAT ALLEY, BILL EXTENSION, G'BRICKSTACK, TRENCH JUNCTION, RYAN'S KEEP & FRANKS KEEP. Orders were received for the relief of two batteries by two batteries of the [illegible] of relocation. MW	
	16/1/17		Our trench Mortar fire drew a certain amount of retaliation from the enemy mortars. The gun emplacements at A.21.d.15.35, A.21.b.70.75, A.21.b.90.95, & A.21.b.70.90. received most attention, but no damage was caused. 134 rounds were fired during the day & night on the usual targets. MW	Battery orders No. 24

A5834. Wt.W4973/M687 750,000 8/16 D. D. & L. Ltd. Forms/C.2118/13.

Army Form C. 2118.

WAR DIARY
or
INTELLIGENCE SUMMARY.
(Erase heading not required.)

Place	Date	Hour	Summary of Events and Information	Remarks and references to Appendices
LE PREOL	17/4/17		The B. Section relieved M.T. Section in the line. MN	
			Stokes Mortars fired 70 rounds during the day & night. The following targets were engaged:- BILL EXTENSION, 'A' BRICKSTACKS, EMBANKMENT REDOUBT, FRANKS KEEP, Trench Junctions & SPOTTED DOG ALLEY. MN	
	18/4/17		Our Trench Mortars fire drew much retaliation when 'H' Brickstacks was fired on. 122 rounds were expended on various targets. MN	
	19/4/17		At 7.45 pm Enemy Trench Mortars has shells were fired on our front trenches. All our guns retaliated. 87 rounds were fired during the day & night. The following targets were engaged: 'H' BRICKSTACKS, FRANKS KEEP, EMBANKMENT REDOUBT, Trench Junctions (A >< C) & BRICKBAT ALLEY. MN	
	20/4/17		Enemy T.M's fired on IKEY TERRACE, HUNTER STREET, HEDGEWARE ROAD. Our T.M's retaliated. 70 rounds were expended & the following targets engaged:- Hostile T.M. 'CAP', TORTOISE, A & B BRICKSTACK. MN	

Army Form C. 2118.

WAR DIARY
or
INTELLIGENCE SUMMARY.
(Erase heading not required.)

Place	Date	Hour	Summary of Events and Information	Remarks and references to Appendices
Le PREOL	20/4/17		Stokes Mortars displaced an enemy working party in the vicinity of FRANKS KEEP. 105 rounds were fired during the day tonight to divert movement and retaliation. Orders issued for the relief of No.2 Section by No.1. MGN	Gallery Drawing No 15.
	21/4/17		No.2 Section relieved No.1 in the line. 1. OR proceed on leave. 125 rounds were fired during the day tonight on the following targets HALSE TMPosition. DUCK'S DEEP, BRICK BAT ALLEY, FRANKS KEEP, FRENCH JUNCTIONS (A23 C.) & BILL EXTENSION. MGN	
	22/4/17		Enemy trench Mortars were very quiet throughout the day tonight. Our Stokes Mortars fired 90 rounds on the usual targets. MGN	
	23/4/17		111 rounds were fired during the day tonight. The enemy heavily retaliated when BILL EXTENSION was fired on. At 7.30pm 500 was discharged on to the enemy trenches, and at intervals until midnight. Our Stokes Mortars Co-(perated) with the feed artillery, and fired 360 rounds on the following targets BILL EXTENSION, TORTOISE	

WAR DIARY
OR
INTELLIGENCE SUMMARY.
(Erase heading not required.)

Army Form C. 2118.

Place	Date	Hour	Summary of Events and Information	Remarks and references to Appendices
Le PREOL	26/4/17		EMBANKMENT REDOUBT, BRICKBAT ALLEY, SPOTTED DOG ALLEY and Trench at A.22 B/5. 22 rounds were fired on Trench Junction (A.22 c & A.28 a). 30 rounds were fired on Trench Junctions A.22 c 8.09, and FRANKS KEEP.	
	26/4/17		Enemy T.M's fired a few rounds during the day and appeared to be searching for our No 3 gun at A.21 B41.30. Our T.M's retaliated. 50 rounds were fired on the following targets:- BILL EXTENSION, BRICK BAT ALLEY, TORTOISE and FRANKS KEEP.	
	27/4/17		Enemy Trench Mortars were slightly more active than yesterday. The areas that received most hostile attentions were in M/S d. Four BRICKSTACKS to RAILWAY EMBANKMENT, A.21 d.18.35 and A.21 b.41.30. Stokes Mortars fired 40 rounds on the usual targets. Orders issued for the relief of Notts & Derby by 2 or retorted to the Battery for duty and taken on strength. Section Relief 7b.6	
	28/4/17		Enemy French Mortars were very quiet. Our Mortars fired 25 rounds in retaliation to hostile T.M. Section relief carried out.	
	29/4/17		Hostile T.M's were very active between 1.0 pm & 3.30 pm. Our guns retaliated with the usual amount of fire. 95 rounds were expended on the following targets: EMBANKMENT REDOUBT	

Army Form C. 2118.

WAR DIARY
or
INTELLIGENCE SUMMARY.
(Erase heading not required.)

Instructions regarding War Diaries and Intelligence Summaries are contained in F. S. Regs., Part II. and the Staff Manual respectively. Title pages will be prepared in manuscript.

Place	Date	Hour	Summary of Events and Information	Remarks and references to Appendices
Le PREOL	30/1/17		Hostile T.M. Aboutloves TORTOISE, BILL EXTENSION, CHATEAU ALLEY and MINE TRENCH 1. O.R. was wounded by shell fire.	
			Hostile T.M.s were fairly active in the afternoon and a fright strung in the vicinity of FINCHLEY ROAD and our BRICKSTACKS. From 9.0p.m to 9.10p.m high Minenwerfer fired gas shells in the proximity of MARYLEBONE TRENCH EDGEWARE ROAD and COLDSTREAM LANE. All our guns retaliated. 370 rounds were fired on the usual targets.	
"	31/1/17		Hostile T.M.s were fairly active in the morning in the vicinity of FINCHLEY ROAD and the first line in A.21.C. and A.27.F. Several shots fell very near our gun emplacements but no damage was done. Our mortars fired 160 rounds on the following targets: BILL EXTENSION, MINE TRENCH, CHATEAU ALLEY, BRICKBAT ALLEY, TORTOISE and N.W.11.BC. BRICKSTACKS.	

M Hamlet Capt.
O.C. 126 Trench Mortar Battery

Army Form C. 2118.

Confidential

WAR DIARY
or
INTELLIGENCE SUMMARY.
(Erase heading not required.)

126th Light Trench Mortar Battery

Volume XI

From Jan 1st 1918 to Jan 31st 1918

Army Form C. 2118.

WAR DIARY
INTELLIGENCE SUMMARY.
(Erase heading not required.)

Instructions regarding War Diaries and Intelligence Summaries are contained in F. S. Regs., Part II. and the Staff Manual respectively. Title pages will be prepared in manuscript.

Place	Date	Hour	Summary of Events and Information	Remarks and references to Appendices
Le PREOL	1/1/18		Hostile T.M's very quiet during the day & night. Stokes Mortars fired 175 rounds on the following targets: — MINE TRENCH, TRENCH JUNCTIONS in A25.c, N8.c.B, RICKSTACKS, TORTOISE, BRICKAT ALLEY. Operation & Administrative Orders received for the relief of the Brigade by the 137. Inf Brigade.	Sector Order No 27
	2/1/18		Battery Order issued for the relief of the Battery by 173. T.M. Battery. Hostile & Own T.M. Hostile Trench Mortars quiet during the day & night. 120 rounds Stokes Bombs were fired on the several targets. 2 O.R. proceed on 14 days leave to U.K. M.O.H.	
	3/1/18		The 173" T.M.Battery relieved the 176" T.M.Battery in the line. The relief commenced at 7:35 p.m. without casualties. On completion of relief the Battery moved to BEUVRY and took over billets. M.H.	
	4/1/18		The Battery paraded at 9 a.m. for general fatigue work at Hughstey trench, both the 1st Bn of Manchester's, in a area of Manchester. 1 O.R. evacuated to the CCS in a state of the strength of the Battery.	

Army Form C. 2118.

WAR DIARY
INTELLIGENCE SUMMARY.
(Erase heading not required.)

Place	Date	Hour	Summary of Events and Information	Remarks and references to Appendices
BEUVRY	3/1/18		Training programme consisting of Musketry, Squad Drill, and Semaphore Signalling and Revolver firing carried out for the day. 2/Lieut Stanton RFC & 2/Lieut A.E.O.R. attended a demonstration at the Army Cookery School.	
	4/1/18		Divine Service in the morning. Educational Training in the afternoon.	
			BETHUNE	
			Capt J.W. Hampson spent the day with No 2 Squadron RFC in the morning.	
	5/1/18		The Battery paraded for bath in the morning. Educational training in the afternoon. 2/Lt W. Maddison spent the day with No 2 Squadron RFC.	
	8/1/18		The Battery celebrated Christmas Day. Dinner to be provided for the men.	
	9/1/18		Lieut Ainsworth and 30 O. Ranks proceeded to Div. R.E. Dumps for Fatigue at 9.0 a.m. Lieut-Bull and 4 O.R's proceeded on leave to U.K. 10/1/18 to 24/1/18. 1 NCO proceeded to Refresher Gas Course at Div. Gas School ESSARS.	

Army Form C. 2118.

WAR DIARY or INTELLIGENCE SUMMARY.

Place	Date	Hour	Summary of Events and Information	Remarks and references to Appendices
BEUVRY	10/1/18		Battery paraded in the morning at 9.0. Training carried out included Musketry, Squad Drill and instruction in the Ahmys Fuze. 1 OR admitted to hospital in England struck off strength. 1 OR taken on strength to complete establishment.	
	11/1/18		3 NCOs and 30 men with Lieut Baldwin in charge reported for fatigue at the Div RE Dump at 9.0 am. 1 OR rejoined from hospital and taken on the attached strength.	
	12/1/18		Orders received for the relief of 125th LTMB by this unit in the line. Training programme carried out during the morning included Physical Training & Bayonet fighting, Musketry, Squad Drill & instruction in the Always Fuze. Lecture for Officers & NCOs in the afternoon on Map Reading. 1 OR reported to the Battery from today.	
	13/1/18		Divine Service in the morning. 2 NCOs + 28 men with Lieut Morris in charge, proceeded for fatigue work on the VILLAGE LINE at 4.0 pm. Battery Operation Orders were issued for the relief of 125th LTMB by this unit. 2 OR reported to the Battery for study to replace 2 OR returned to unit. 2 OR rejoined the Battery from leave.	Battery Orders No 28

Army Form C. 2118.

WAR DIARY
or
INTELLIGENCE SUMMARY.
(Erase heading not required.)

Instructions regarding War Diaries and Intelligence Summaries are contained in F. S. Regs., Part II. and the Staff Manual respectively. Title pages will be prepared in manuscript.

Place	Date	Hour	Summary of Events and Information	Remarks and references to Appendices
BEUVRY	14/1/18		Orders received for the postponement of the relief of 125th RTMB by this Unit until further orders. Battery Paraded at 11.0 am for lecture on the Always Fuze & inspection of Gas Masks. Recreational Training carried out in afternoon	
	15/1/18		Training carried out during morning included Physical Training & Bayonet fighting, Squad & Ceremonial Drill & Gas Drill with Gas Masks. Lecture for Officers & NCOs at 5 p.m. on Map Reading. Orders received for the relief of 125th RTM Battery by the 175th Inst. Battery Operation Orders revised accordingly & issued. 2 OR reported to the Battery for duty & taken on attached strength.	
	16/1/18		1 NCO & 25 OR with Lt Baldwin in charge proceeded to the Div. RE. Dump at 9.0 am for fatigue work. Lieut. Ainsworth & Cpt Fisher proceeded to the 1st Corps School (CHARMEUX) to attend an instruction course on Stokes Mortars. Amendments to Battery Operation orders issued. An advance party of 2 NCO's & 8 men proceeded to the line to take over positions	

Army Form C. 2118.

WAR DIARY
INTELLIGENCE SUMMARY.
(Erase heading not required.)

Place	Date	Hour	Summary of Events and Information	Remarks and references to Appendices
BEUVRY	17/1/18		Battery paraded at 8.30am and marched to FESTUBERT. Took over fm Hqrs from 125th L TM Bty. Relief completed by 2.30pm without casualties. 2.OR returned to the Battery for duty & taken on attached strength. 1 OR joined the Battery from hospital taken on attached strength. 2 OR proceeded on Lewis gun course at 1st Corps School. 1 OR CHATEAU-ST-PRY.	
FESTUBERT	18/1/18		Enemy TMs very quiet during day & night. Our Mortars fired 12 Rounds on AUSTRIAN TRENCH in retaliation to enemy T.M. fire. 2OR proceeded on 14 days leave to U.K. 6OR on fatigue with R.Es.	A.9.C.76.90.
	19/1/18		2OR proceeded on 14 days leave fm pit at A.9.C.76.90. Nothing much fm Enemy quiet. Our mortars fired twenty (20) rounds were fired by our Mortars on A.9.58.76 (Suspected M.G. Emplacement) in retaliation to enemy TM fire. 6 OR on fatigue with R.Es building new gun pit at A.9.C.76.90.	
	20/1/18		Enemy Mortars more active than on previous 3 days. Our Heavy mortars & medium mortar fire drew strong retaliation on GIVENCHY RIDGE & AUSTRIAN WAY (A.9.580.12) Our Mortars fired 20 rounds in retaliation on AUSTRIAN WAY (A.9.580.12). 2 OR Returned from 14 days leave to UK. 2 OR returned from Alloways Gun course.	new fm pit A9 C.76.90.

WAR DIARY or INTELLIGENCE SUMMARY

Army Form C. 2118.

Place	Date	Hour	Summary of Events and Information	Remarks and references to Appendices
FESTUBERT	21/1/18		Enemy's light mortars fired on SCOTTISH TRENCH UPPER CUT TRENCH and WOOD LANE. Our Mortars retaliated with 140 rounds on the following targets. A9 b 30.42. A9 b 66.66. MACKENSEN TRENCH. and A10 c. 30.60. Battery HQs moved from FESTUBERT to a farm at F4 a 60.17 (Sorry) Move complete at 5.15 pm. New gun pit at A9C76.90 Carried on with MMA	
GORRE (F4 a 60.17)	22/1/18		Enemy TMs quiet. In retaliation to hostile H.T.M on Mortars fired 13 rounds on SAXON WAY (Trench Junction) A10. C. 12. 68. Hostile H.T.M craved fire. Work carried on improving gun emplacement. New pit at A9C76.90 almost complete. MMA	
	23/1/18		A shift of the gun teams in the line was carried out in the morning. Without casualties. Enemy TMs very quiet during day & night. Our mortars fired 12 rounds on S.O.S lines during the night on the Right-Batt-Front Work carried on cleaning ammunition & improving gun pits. MMA	Orders No 29
	24/1/18		Hostile TMS very quiet. No retaliation work carried on with at the new SOS gun emplacement (A3 a 52.76) L/Cpl Jones proceeded for a Course to the Brigade School (B+ P T Class) Pt GORRE proceeded for a Course to the Brigade Salvage Section. MMA	

WAR DIARY / INTELLIGENCE SUMMARY

Army Form C. 2118.

Place	Date	Hour	Summary of Events and Information	Remarks and references to Appendices
GORRE (F+a.b.0.17)	25/1/18		Hostile TMs fired a few light bombs on AVENUE TRENCH. We retaliated with 12 rounds on MACKENSEN TRENCH (A3.a.55.70) The S.O.S. gun emplacement under reconstruction at A3.a.55.70 complete. MMA	
	26/1/18		Enemy Mortars very quiet all day except for a few light rounds which fell in the proximity of GIVENCHY KEEP. Our mortar retaliated with 18 rounds from A.10.a.31.70 (Queen junction). Hostile Mortar ceased fire. Lieut. Bull + 4 OR rejoined the Battery from leave. MMA	
	27/1/18		Hostile TMs were fairly active on area A9C from 9.30 am to 10.30 am. In retaliation 30 rounds were fired on A10 c 15.60 (Trench junction) and MACKENSEN TRENCH. (A9 c.H.6.70). Work proceeded with our new S.O.S. emplacement at A9C 76.90. 1 OR proceeded on 14 days leave to UK. MMA	
	28/1/18		Hostile TMs active. A number of rounds were fired in the vicinity of KINGS ROAD and GIVENCHY KEEP and also to the right of the Brigade front. Our Mortars retaliated with 40 rounds on MACKENSEN TRENCH A9C 30.42. A9d 46.70. A9d 65.77. Work carried on salving ammunition. 2 OR proceeded on 14 days leave 6 UK. MMA	

WAR DIARY
INTELLIGENCE SUMMARY.
(Erase heading not required.)

Army Form C. 2118.

Place	Date	Hour	Summary of Events and Information	Remarks and references to Appendices
GORRE (FRABOIS)	29/1/16		A relief of the gun teams in the line was carried out in the morning without casualties. Hostile TM's were quiet. In retaliation to Enemy TM fire in the region of GIVENCHY KEEP our mortars fired 30 rounds on MACKENSEN TRENCH. Work carried on improving emplacements. (AHH)	Battery Order No 30
	30/1/16		Hostile TM's fairly quiet. In retaliation to Enemy TM fire, our mortars fired 25 rounds on CRATER TRENCH, AUSTIN WAY and ANTIC TRENCH. 1 OR killed in action & struck off strength of Unit. Work carried on at the new emplacement at A9c 76.90. & reconstruction of ammunition dumps. (AHH)	
	31/1/16		Hostile TM's very quiet. In retaliation to Enemy TM fire on CALEDONIAN ROAD, WOOD LANE and PRINCESS ISLAND our mortars cooperated with the Medium Mortars 40 rounds being expended on MACKENSEN TRENCH and ANTIC TRENCH. (A9c). (AHH)	

M Humphreys Capt
O/C 176 T.M.B.

WAR DIARY
or
INTELLIGENCE SUMMARY.

(Erase heading not required.)

Army Form C. 2118.

126th Light Trench Mortar Battery.

Volume XII

From Feb 1st 1918 to Feb. 28th 1918

Army Form C. 2118.

WAR DIARY
or
INTELLIGENCE SUMMARY.

Ref Sheets 36aSE4 36SW3 36CNW1 36SNE2

(Erase heading not required.)

Instructions regarding War Diaries and Intelligence Summaries are contained in F. S. Regs., Part II. and the Staff Manual respectively. Title pages will be prepared in manuscript.

Place	Date	Hour	Summary of Events and Information	Remarks and references to Appendices
GORRE.	1/2/18		Hostile T.M's were very quiet during the night and day. In cooperation with our Medium T.M's our mortars fired 25 rounds on MACKENSON TRENCH, AUSTRIAN WAY and PRUSSIAN WAY. Work carried on with new S.O.S. pit at AP.C 76.90, and improvement of ammunition dumps. Original copy of War Diary sent to H.Q. 1. O.R. killed in action.	
"	2/2/18		Hostile T.M's very quiet. Our light mortars fired 20 rounds neutralising fire on the junction of SUNKEN ROAD TRENCH and MACKENSON TRENCH. The Lieutenant carried on. Ammunition in the forward trenches overhauled. Battery plan issued for the relief of tomorrow.	Hostile plan 7/1/2
"	3/2/18		Hostile T.M's more active on the left battalion front. Relieved tomorrow 15-19 rounds heavy T.M. 1 light T.M. fell at the junction of PIONEER R? COVER TRENCH. 19 rounds light T.M. in COVER TRENCH on the right battalion front. Hostile mortars were very quiet. 1 OR killed in action. FRIDAY WALK 10 rounds on AP.d.09.75, 2nd Lt gunner. 2 rounds fell in enemy A.10.a.31.10. Junction line and 2 rounds on SAXON WAY, PRUSSIAN WAY, Trench junction AP.d.90.62 2/Lieut AINSWORTH and 2 O.R. rejoined de Gaudry from T.M. Course at the 1st Army School.	
"	4/2/18		Hostile T.M. very quiet on the right Batt front. A few rounds fell on the batt. lost front. (Line relieved)	

CONFIDENTIAL. B.M.C.22/71.

Headquarters,
    42nd. Division.

    Herewith War Diaries of the following units for the month of February 1918.

    126th. Infy. Bde. Headquarters.

    1/5th. E. Lancs. Regt.

    1/8th. Manchester Regt.

    1/10th. Manchester Rgt.

    126th. L.T.M. Battery.

    Please acknowledge receipt.

C. B. Dyson
Lieut.
for
    Brig-General,
    Commanding 126th. Infy. Bde.

5/3/18.

WAR DIARY or INTELLIGENCE SUMMARY

Army Form C. 2118.

Place	Date	Hour	Summary of Events and Information	Remarks and references to Appendices
TORRE	5/2/18		Held M.T. more lightly than in the previous days on the right. Battalion front. At night 11 M's fell in COVENTRY LAP, PICCADILLY and MENIN TRENCH. On the left battn front 8 KAMERADWERFER shots fired on BARNTON TRENCH N.E. & light M.T. fell in S.27.b.8.90. Our light mortars fired 18 rounds on AUSTRIAN WAY PRUSSIAN WAY SAXON WAY Front line in sq.d.	
"	6/2/18		Enemy M.T. quieter on left def front. Slightly more active on right. Our light mortars fired 10 rounds on retaliation, scattering fire on MACDONSON TRENCH, SAXON WAY. Front line in sq.d. Work carried on work emplacement along drainage.	
"	7/2/18		Held T.M's very quiet all day. Work carried on work emplacement sq Mo 76.90.	
"	8/2/18		Held T.M's quiet. During the day & night our light mortars fired 30 rounds on MACDENSON TRENCH Sec 9 rounds on a bobbed stoke "L" Lap. Enemy emcubits fixed down a rifle during barrage gun the Bdescen Lgt S.Inft and SCOTTISH TRENCH as far as PRINCES ISLAND. 1 O.R. proceeded on leave to U.K.	

WAR DIARY or INTELLIGENCE SUMMARY

Army Form C. 2118.

Place	Date	Hour	Summary of Events and Information	Remarks and references to Appendices
GORRE	9/7/18		Mobile T.M's quiet. 30 light bombs fell in the vicinity of COVER TRENCH, PIONEER Tr and BARNTON SOUTH. In co-operation with the infantry our mortars fired 26 rounds on AUSTRIAN WAY, PRUSSIAN WAY, SAXON WAY and DOVER TRENCH for dispersing enemy working party.	Battery Orders No. 22
"	10/7/18		Enemy Heavy Mortar very quiet. Our mortars fired 20 rounds on MACHENSON Tr, SUNKEN ROAD TRENCH and DOVER TRENCH. Work carried on and new emplacement at A96. 76.90	
"	11/7/18		10 light T.M. fell on GIVENCHY REDOUBT. At 6.15 pm the right battalion carried out a raid. During the operation 2 of our mortars fired 23 rounds. A barrage was put down on SUNKEN ROAD TRENCH from a point A96.70.40 passing through A96 30.35 to A96.65.45. A steady fire was also maintained on the enemy front line from A3d 62.30 to A96. 70.65. 2 OR proceeded on 14 days leave to U.K.	
"	12/7/18		Operation Orders Administration and instructions received for the relief of the Brigade by the 105th Inf Brigade. Battery orders issued for the relief of the Battery by the 105th L.T.M. Battery. Mobile T.M's very quiet, since the raid of the previous evening. Our mortars fired 68 rounds on the usual targets in retaliation to hostile fire.	Battery Orders No. 123

Army Form C. 2118.

WAR DIARY
or
INTELLIGENCE SUMMARY.
(Erase heading not required.)

Place	Date	Hour	Summary of Events and Information	Remarks and references to Appendices
GORE	13/7/18		Morale T.M. very quiet. One Your guns at L.27.K.92.93 was put out of action by a 77.mm at 5.15 a.m. OA	
	14/7/18		The 165th (A/M.R) relieved the 176th Bgde in the line. Relief completed by 12.30 p.m. On completion of relief the Battery marched to BUSNES.	
GORE and BUSNES.			Arrived at BUSNES at 7.30 p.m. and took over billets. No overhead fire put on the line of march. OA	
"	15/7/18		The Battery rested during the day. Paid the men in the afternoon. Orders received for the attached men of the "A" Frame 2/9" Mcr High to rejoin their unit. OA	
"	16/7/18		Cleaning equipment etc general fatigues. 10.00 proceeded to rejoin their units. Lt. R.L. Packman & "Game" Reg. rejoined the Battery from leave. CO conference at 19.H. at 4.30 p.m. ONH	
"	17/7/18		The Battery paraded for Divine Service at 10.30 a.m. at the Recreation Room BUSNES. The Battery paraded for bath at 3.30 p.m. OA	

Army Form C. 2118.

WAR DIARY
or
INTELLIGENCE SUMMARY.
(Erase heading not required.)

Place	Date	Hour	Summary of Events and Information	Remarks and references to Appendices
BUSNES	19/3/18		Training carried out for the day consisted of Ceremonial Drill Bayonet fighting, Squad Drill Musketry. 1. OR reported to Gordon from leave. JOA	
	20/3/18		Battery paraded for Squad Drill Physical Bayonet fighting, Ceremonial Drill in the morning. Tel. instruction in the afternoon. Lecture to officers NCO's in the evening. JOA	
	21/3/18		Training in the morning consisted of Gun Drill Gas Drill, Ceremonial Drill Half Holiday in the afternoon. JOA	
	22/3/18		Daily training programme carried out. Battery paraded for talks on the afternoon. JOA	
	23/3/18		Training for the day consisted of Battery Drill Ceremonial Drill Physical Bayonet fighting, Musketry, Lecture in the evening for officers. 1. OR attended 223 Amb. 1 OR taken on strength of Battery & complete establishment. 16 reinforcements proceeded to UK on 10 days leave. Paid the men of the Battery. JOA	

WAR DIARY
or
INTELLIGENCE SUMMARY.
(Erase heading not required.)

Army Form C. 2118.

Place	Date	Hour	Summary of Events and Information	Remarks and references to Appendices
BUSNES	23/7/18		Training for the morning consisted of Battery Drill, Gun laying by compass. Football in the afternoon. 2 OR admitted Field Ambulance.	
	24/7/18		The Battery paraded at 11 am for Divine Service. 1 OR rejoined the Battery from leave.	
	25/7/18		The Battery paraded for Battery Drill (Gremencourt Drill Mindery) in the morning and for Bayonet fighting Drum Drill in the afternoon. 1 OR rejoined from leave and 1 OR rejoined from hospital.	
	26/7/18		The Battery paraded at 8.45 am & proceeded by Lorry to the 1st Corps Small Motor Range at GOSNAY for live firing.	
	27/7/18		The Battery paraded at 9 am for tactical scheme. Recreational training in the afternoon. 1 OR admitted to Hosp. 1 OR rejoined from hospital taken in attached strength. 1 OR admitted to Hosp.	
	28/7/18		Training for the day consisted of Battery Drill (Gun fire Gremencourt Drill Mindery). The Machine Officer inspected the men of the Battery. 1 OR admitted to Hosp.	

A Hunter Capt.
O.C. 176 fMb Battery

42nd Division.
126th Infantry Brigade.

126th LIGHT TRENCH MORTAR BATTERY

MARCH 1 9 1 8

Army Form C. 2118.

WAR DIARY
or
INTELLIGENCE SUMMARY.
(Erase heading not required.)

126th Light Trench Mortar Battery

Volume XIII

From March 1st 1918 to March 31st 1918.

Army Form C. 2118.

WAR DIARY
or
INTELLIGENCE SUMMARY.
(Erase heading not required.)

Place	Date	Hour	Summary of Events and Information	Remarks and references to Appendices
BUSNES	1/3/18		Training for the day consisted of Physical, Major's & fighting Gun Drill. Attending with Officers Morton, Laughton, Signalling Refresher Lectures. War Diary for February sent to R.H.A. JDH	
"	2/3/18		Orders received for the Brigade to reinforce the Portuguese. Two motor lorries reported to Battery H.Qrs to convey stores & gun teams to Battery H.Qrs at ZELOBES. The Battery moved off at 11-30 am. H.Qrs arrived at ZELOBES at 1-30 pm. Capt A.J. Hampton reported to Brigade M.Qrs for instructions. Reinforcement not required. The Battery returned to BUSNES and took over billets. JDH	
"	3/3/18		No training carried out during the day. Operation and Manoeuvre Order received for the move of the Brigade to BURBURE area, and take over from the 127th [?] Bde Brigade. Battery orders issued for the move to BURBURE and to relieve the 127th How[itzer] Battery 2 [?] orders JDH	Battery orders 24
BUSNES & BURBURE	4/3/18		Advance party 1 Off & 1 N.C.O proceeded to BURBURE at 9 am to take over billets from the 127th Lt How Battery. The Battery paraded at 12-45 pm and marched to new area. Arrived at BURBURE at 3 pm and took over billets. JDH	

WAR DIARY or INTELLIGENCE SUMMARY

Army Form C. 2118.

Place	Date	Hour	Summary of Events and Information	Remarks and references to Appendices
BURBURE	5/2/18		Training for the day consisted of Musketry, Ceremonial Drill and Saluting, Gun Drill, Lewis Gun, Semaphore Signalling & Recreational Training.	
"	6/2/18		The Battn: paraded at 9 a.m. for Instructional Réference on flying. Lieut. Morton at ton flying aeroplane.	
"	7/2/18		Training for the day consisted of drill, Bayonet training, Lewis Gun drill, Squad & extended order, & instruction regarding the preparation of baking barrels for actual scheme and the Coy will be round in turn. Most returned a lecture at 6.30 pm by the Divisional Commander.	
"	8/2/18		The Battery attended the Lessons of Staff Sergt. Sutsoola M.M. for burning. The men stood in the afternoon.	
"	9/2/18		2 Officers proceeded at 6.30 am by lorry to the VERMELLES area for reconnaissance purposes. The Battalion paraded at 9 am for baths at lower.	

WAR DIARY or INTELLIGENCE SUMMARY

Army Form C. 2118.

Place	Date	Hour	Summary of Events and Information	Remarks and references to Appendices
BURBURE	10/3/18		The Battery attended Divine Service. Football match in the afternoon. JMcA	
"	11/3/18		Trained for the day consisted of Physical training beyond Toglov, Gas Drill, McLine scheme with live fuses. Lt H Marsden proceeded on leave to UK. JMcA	
"	12/3/18		Training programme carried out consisted of Physical training, Gunnery, Gas descriptive lecture, Wireless lecture. Wgt L Ward in Portchester. 2. OR proceeded on 14 days leave to UK. Lt Hurworth rejoined the Battery from leave. JMcA	
"	13/3/18		The Battery paraded for Physical training Monday to Saturday. Heavy Drill Recreational training in the afternoon. JMcA	
"	14/3/18		Orders received at 6.30 am for the Brigade to "Stand by" prepare to move. The Battery ready to move off by 1 pm. Move cancelled. In the afternoon training was proceeded with. The Battery paraded in line for any drill. JMcA	
"	15/3/18		The Battery paraded for bath at S Souval Livers. On return the usual training was carried out. 1 OR rejoined the Battery from hospital. JMcA	

WAR DIARY
or
INTELLIGENCE SUMMARY.

Army Form C. 2118.

Place	Date	Hour	Summary of Events and Information	Remarks and references to Appendices
BURBURE	16/3/18		Training for the day consisted of Physical Bayonet exercises & Gas Drill. HM instructors who were on leave during the morning. Reinforced training & Musketry Lecture in the afternoon. 1 Off. & 9 N.C.O. attended a lecture on the Church Army Hut Services at 3 p.m. 2 OR taken on the strength of the Battn to complete establishment. The battery paraded at 10 a.m. for Divine Service in the YMCA.	
	17/3/18		Reinforced training in the afternoon.	
	18/3/18		Training programme for the day consisted of Physical Bayonet training. Bomb Drill, Musketry Drill. Map Reading (reading a contour map). 2 OR rejoined the Battery from leave.	
	19/3/18		Training programme for the day carried out. 4 OR proceeded on leave to U.K. 1 OR rejoined from hospital.	
	20/3/18		Training proceeded with. Reinforced training in the afternoon. 1 Off. & 21 OR attended a lecture at Lozinghem at 2.30 p.m. 2 OR proceeded on leave to U.K. 2 OR rejoined this week.	
	21/3/18		Training programme for the day consisted of Physical Bayonet fighting, Arms Drill, Map Reading Musketry (rapid practice).	

WAR DIARY
INTELLIGENCE SUMMARY
(Erase heading not required.)

Army Form C. 2118.

Place	Date	Hour	Summary of Events and Information	Remarks and references to Appendices
BURBURE	27/3/18		Training in the morning consisted of Bayonet fighting + Lewis Drill. Line firing carried out in the afternoon. Had the news of the Battery and the move of the Brigade to afford Div. of M.R.R. Orders issued for the move of the Brigade to afford. Conference held at M.R.R. re above Orders issued to have all stores ready for removal. 30ft	
"	23/3/18		The Brigade moved from BURBURE by French the Battery formed at P.15.a.w. march. 16 ammunition found in the KEEPERS ROAD proceeded to ADINFER WOOD. Grooms here arrived & & furn stayed the night. 30ft	
ADINFER WOOD	24/3/18		Orders received for the Brigade to proceed to the line. The Battery harnessed at 2 then an fighting order marched to LOGEAST WOOD had tea and harnessed in the wood till dusk. The Brigade received orders to go on Divisional Reserve. The Battery left LOGEAST WOOD at 9.30 pm and marched to RAILWAY CUTTING nr COURCELLES. The Germans	
LOGEAST WOOD			attacked our positions the Brigade stood to. 30ft	
RAILWAY CUTTING N'COURCELLES	25/3/18		The morning passed quietly. In the afternoon the enemy started a heavy bombardment & attacked. The Railway cutting was heavily shelled. We had to retire because Leave the Battery and count General connection. Situation became	

A.534 Wt.W4973/M657 750,000 8/16 D. D. & L. Ltd. Forms/C.2118/13.

WAR DIARY
INTELLIGENCE SUMMARY

Army Form C. 2118.

Place	Date	Hour	Summary of Events and Information	Remarks and references to Appendices
ABLAINZEVILLE	26/3/18		Sent a patrol of 1 NCO & 3 men to find touch with the Battalion on the left. The patrol returned & communication established. Orders received for the Brigade to withdraw to ABLAINZEVILLE. OKH	
	27/3/18		Btn. L. saw the Enemy walking from the cutting to ABLAINZEVILLE. Patrol found one the CHATEAU. Orders passed to move at 6. 30am to BUCQUOY. On the Battn. arrival to a sunken road in rear of the village, relieved the day long action. Enemy guns (village, relieved the day long action. Enemy guns (Enemy tanks) a terrific bombardment in the morning & attacks Enemy artillery repeated firing artillery enhance very our time. The attack was repelled. Enemy shelling heavy gradual & sundry trench close throughout the evening. Enemy shelling heavy gradual & sundry the enemy. The activity across enemy the many of the coy/Bn had from left ran. The activity actually covers the many of the coy/Bn had from left withdraw to trenches in ESSART. OKH	
ESSARTS LES BUCQUOY	28/3/18		Enemy artillery very active in open ground. The Factory received orders to take of guns at the disposal of the Battalion on the line. This order was cancelled later. OKH	
	29/3/18		Orders received for the relief of the Battn by the 1st Bn Res. The Brigade moved back to ESSART on occupied trenches. OKH	

Army Form C. 2118.

WAR DIARY
or
INTELLIGENCE SUMMARY.
(Erase heading not required.)

Place	Date	Hour	Summary of Events and Information	Remarks and references to Appendices
ESSARTS LES BUCQUOY	2/9/16		Enemy artillery fairly quiet on back areas. The weather warmer & more fine at intervals.	
	3/9/16		The weather continues warmer. Enemy artillery quite to normal. Our artillery active at intervals during the day & night.	

J.W.W. Fraser Capt.
O.C. 176 L.T.M. Battery

Battery Operation Order No 3.4.
Ref 36A 1/40000

1. The 126th LTM Battery will relieve the 127th LTM Battery at BURBURE on the 4th inst.

2. Route will be via LILLERS and MENSECQ. The starting point will be Road Junction U5d 70.35 — time 1pm.

3. 8 Guns less boxes & spare parts will be handed over to the 127th LTM Bty at LE PIRE

3/3/19   Signed H.J. HAMPSON
                          Capt
                     OC 126 LTMB

Administrative Instruction in accordance with O.O. No 34.

1. Railhead remains at LILLERS
2. Refilling Point at HAUT RIEUX approx U.23.d.8.2 from the 5th inst. The exact locality will be notified later. The hour for refilling will be at 9.0 am.
3. Supplies. Rations for the 4 & 5th inst will be drawn on the 3rd and carried on the Motor Lorry. Rations for the 6th will be drawn on the 5th. Refilling point new area
4. Transport. One Lorry will be available which if necessary will make two journeys.
5. Billeting Parties 1 off + 1 NCO to report to the 127th LTMB Hqrs to take over billets
6. Stores. Receipts for Stores handed over in to incoming units will be obtained in duplicate.
7. Rear Party. 1 NCO + 1 OR will remain behind + obtain necessary certificates as regards cleanliness of billets etc handed over.
8. DADOS Remains at BUSNES

Location of hostile trench
was as nearly as possible ascertained
after taking over.

8/3/18

Signed H J HARRISON
Capt
136 L.T.M. Battery

126th Inf.Bde.
42nd Div.

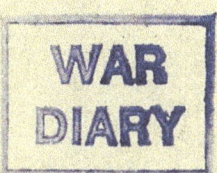

126th LIGHT TRENCH MORTAR BATTERY.

A P R I L

1 9 1 8

Attached:
Appendices.

Army Form C. 2118.

WAR DIARY
or
INTELLIGENCE SUMMARY.
(Erase heading not required.)

126th Light Trench Mortar Battery.

Volume XIV

From April 1st 1918 to April 30th 1918.

Place	Date	Hour	Summary of Events and Information	Remarks and references to Appendices
ESSARTS LES BREQUOY	1/4/18		Enemy artillery very active on back areas. The trenches in vicinity (ESSARTS) shelled rather heavily during the afternoon. Orders received for the Brigade to relieve a Brigade of the 41st Div in the front line. The Battery received orders to place 2 guns at the disposal of each battalion in the line. 3 Officers proceeded to the line to reconnoitre. The gun teams proceeded to (select) position at 9.0 p.m. M.M.	
	2/4/18		We moved 4 all guns was completed by 5.0 am. 2 guns being installed on each battalion front. Enemy aeroplanes normally active on each battalion front. Enemy aeroplanes normally active. LOS emplacements and work carried on with the construction of emplacements and ammunition recess. The guns on the right battalion front were withdrawn to conform to new line. M.M.	
	3/4/18		The enemy shelled our forward systems intermittently during the day and night. Enemy aeroplanes extremely active in recce. complete. Gun emplacement ammunition recess complete. Orders received for the relief of the Brigade by the 139th Inf. Brigade. Casualties for the day were (1 O.R. wounded), 1 O.R. missing. Capt. Harrison rejoined from leave. M.M.	Battery Orders No. 35

WAR DIARY or INTELLIGENCE SUMMARY.

Army Form C. 2118.

Place	Date	Hour	Summary of Events and Information	Remarks and references to Appendices
ESSARTS LES BUCQUOY	4/4/18		Enemy activity normal. The trenches in vicinity of ESSARTS received the usual attention. One officer from the 127th MGB reported to Battery HQrs to take over the relieving procedure proceeded to the line at 7. Opm. JM/L	
PIGEON WOOD	5/4/18		Relief completed at 12.15am. The Battery on completion of relief moved to trenches in PIGEON WOOD. The Brigade now in Divisional Reserve. Men worked on modern trestled fatigues. JM/L	
"	6/4/18		Usual recon working fatigues. Orders received for the relief of the Brigade by the 185th Inf. Brigade. 1 Officer reported to the Battery from the 185th Inf. Bde. 2am B. to take over. Brigade met the relieving unit. JM/L	Battery Order No. 36.
SOUASTRE	7/4/18		Relief complete at the Battery on completion of relief moved to SOUASTRE and took over billets. Arrived there at 9. am. Had breakfast then rested during the morning. Orders received for the Brigade to move to MS and HENU. The Battery paraded at 1. Opm and marched to HENU and took over billets. JM/L	Battery Order No. 37.

WAR DIARY or INTELLIGENCE SUMMARY.

Army Form C. 2118.

(Erase heading not required.)

Place	Date	Hour	Summary of Events and Information	Remarks and references to Appendices
HENU	9/11/8		The day spent in general cleaning up. JMT	
"	10/11/8		Men rested during the day. Equipment inspected. Kit inspection. JMT	
"	11/11/8		Light training consisting of Physical Drill Arm Drill & Ceremonial Drill carried out in the morning. The Battery standing for bathe in the afternoon. Gun Teams ready to move at 2 hours notice. JMT	
"	12/11/8		Men cleaned up equipment clothing in the morning. The Ceremonial Ceremonies inspected the Brigade at PHQ at 2.30pm JMT	
"	13/11/8		Light training carried out for the day consisting of Physical & Bayonet fighting, Steady Drill Ceremonial Drill Musketry Training. JMT	
"	14/11/8		The Battery paraded for a route march in the morning. Foot-ball in the afternoon. JMT	
"	15/11/8		Divine Service in the morning. The Battery moved into field billets. JMT	

WAR DIARY or INTELLIGENCE SUMMARY

Army Form C. 2118.

Place	Date	Hour	Summary of Events and Information	Remarks and references to Appendices
HEBUTERNE	14/4/16		Orders received for the relief of the 67th Bde Brigade by the 62nd Inf Brigade	
"	15/4/16		Administrative Orders received for the relief. Warning Orders issued for the relief of the 67th Inf Bde Battery. The Battery paraded for inspection at 2.30 pm by the C.O. 1700 hours proceeded to GOMMECOURT. The Battery paraded at 5.30 pm in fighting order and moved to GOMMECOURT WOOD (near Fonquevillers). Gun teams met & horses provided by the teams relieved gun teams of the 67th I. Mob. Relief completed at 10.30 pm without casualties. Hostile trench mortars active. He enemy shelled in the vicinity of GOMMECOURT WOOD during the day.	Battery Order No 38
LITTLE GOMMECOURT WOOD	16/4/16		A round of M[unition] ammunition carried up to the guns at night. Work carried out making shelters for guns teams. Evening 9PM. 7h2 A.S 12.15 pm C. Stokes Mortar was looked forward into stall, No.5. E. G. half took to be mounted at L.O. G.B. at point Albert. Lts. [signature] ... Rev Mann RSC	

A5834 Wt W4973/M687 750,000 8/16 D. D. & L. Ltd. Forms/C.2118/13.

Army Form C. 2118.

WAR DIARY
or
INTELLIGENCE SUMMARY.

(Erase heading not required.)

Place	Date	Hour	Summary of Events and Information	Remarks and references to Appendices
LINE NR POPPERINGHE WOOD	9/11/16		Emplacement dug at L.7.a.75.20. 150 rds. of ammunition were carried to forward positions (on front). 100 rounds of ammunition were carried to forward positions (U. district on front) [illegible] at L.1.C.b.2 inches SUNKEN ROAD. Orders issued for relief of gun teams. [initials]	Battery Order No. 89
"	10/11/16		A relieving party of men carried out during the night without casualties. Enemy sent Minenwerfer M-bomb over emplacement throwing ammunition. [initials]	
"	11/11/16		Three Minenwerfer fell over L.7.a.75.20. One of our guns was relocated. 100 rounds of ammunition was carried forward to the SUNKEN ROAD at L.12.a.75.70. 100 rounds of ammunition were carried forward from the Brigade dump. New gun position reconnoitred. [initials]	
"	20/11/16		2 enemy T.M's very quiet during the night. Our mortars in L.7.a. were withdrawn to rear positions on the SUNKEN ROAD (KLd.). In addition to this emplacement were improved and ammunition stored in each emplacement. [initials] Enemy medium T.M's fired 5 rounds in afternoon at L.6.C.b.75. In retaliation	
"	21/11/16			

Army Form C. 2118.

WAR DIARY
or
INTELLIGENCE SUMMARY.
(Erase heading not required.)

Place	Date	Hour	Summary of Events and Information	Remarks and references to Appendices
LINE THE SOMMECOURT WOOD	27/4/18		One of our plough mortars fired 15 rounds on K.12.c.19.09. (trench junction) Work carried on improving new emplacement and carrying ammunition. JH. During this morning enemy heavy T.M. fired a few rounds on nearly dry trench running from K.6.a.35.30 to K.6.c.25.90. A few light minnenwerfer fell in & about K.12.b.50.90 and the SUNKEN ROAD (K.6.d.) Our mortars fired 35 rounds on K.7.c.15.20.(trench junction) and K.12.d.70.75. (SUNKEN ROAD) Work carried out camouflaging gun pits, breaking ammunition recess pattern orderbond for the plugs of gun teams. The relief was carried out without casualties. JH	Artillery Order No. 40.
	28/4/18		Enemy T.M. very quiet. 2 new emplacements commenced to be dug in JULIUS POINT at E.28.d.82.95. and K.28.c.78.00. 200 rounds ammunition carried to each of the above emplacements. JH	
"	29/4/18		Enemy T.M. inactive. Gun emplacement in JULIUS POINT (E.28.d.8.9.) completed and gun mounted. Gun emplacement E.28.K.00.90. in the same strong point nearly completed. Ammunition was collected from E.30.C.00.16. and E.29.d.3.3. and dumped in SALMON TRENCH at K.6.a.3.2. JH	

WAR DIARY
INTELLIGENCE SUMMARY

Army Form C. 2118.

Place	Date	Hour	Summary of Events and Information	Remarks and references to Appendices
LINE GOMMECOURT	25/4/18		Hostile T.M's fired 2 Stokes Mortars have been placed in position in K.6.a.79.20 and K.6.a.28.15. Work on these emplacements was carried on. Orders received for intendion relief.	Batt'n Orders No 11
	26/4/18		Enemy T.M's quiet. Work carried on on cemetery emplacement at K.6.a.79.20 and K.6.a.28.15. A relief of the gun teams in the line was carried out during the night without casualties. JM	
	27/4/18		Light Minenwerfer fires on K.6.d. 75.30 and L.7.a 25.15. Our mortars fired 105 rounds on the following targets:- Trench K.12.a 75.25, L.7.c. 0.8, and L.7.c.1.8. O.T. L.7. c.3.7. Astride posts at L.7.c.52.46. L.7.c.60.45, L.7.c.2.46 and Astride M.G. at L.7.a. 60.40. At 6.0 p.m. E.A fired last over Sunken R'd in K.6.d of L.1.c. firing a M.G. One of our mortars fired 3 rounds at the place which silenced and immediately fired back to by our lines. 200 rounds of ammunition were carried forward. Improvement of emplacements at K.6.a 79.20, + K.6.a. 28.15 carried out. JM	
	28/4/18		Enemy T.M's very quiet. At 7.0 p.m a stokes Mortar was taken forward & placed in a shell hole 49 yards (more fire) on trench running from M.12.d.42.8	

Army Form C. 2118.

WAR DIARY
or
INTELLIGENCE SUMMARY.
(Erase heading not required.)

Instructions regarding War Diaries and Intelligence Summaries are contained in F.S. Regs., Part II. and the Staff Manual respectively. Title pages will be prepared in manuscript.

Place	Date	Hour	Summary of Events and Information	Remarks and references to Appendices
LINE WOOD Gommecourt Wood	29/11/18		h.12.d.65.85 and h.12.d.65.60. 200 rounds were carried forward. JDH Enemy MG's fired a few rounds on h.6.c.19 between 8 & 9am. Our mortars fired 30 rounds on enemy trenches h.12.d. and h.12.d.7.6 where a hostile working party was reported. 2 E.A. flew low over our lines on the brigade front during the morning. They were immediately fired on by our mortars and driven off. Work carried on cleaning Underwood & improvement of emplacements. JDH	
"	30/11/18		At intervals during the day trench mortars fired on area h.6.C. 20.95. Our mortars fired 40 rounds on enemy front at L.7.C. 15.65. Work carried on improving front line & emplacement. Orders received for relief by N.Z. Rifle Brigade. JDH	Battery relieved. No cas.

[signatures]

OC 176 LTM Battery

APPENDICES.

Battery Operation Order No 35.

1. On the night of the 4/5th inst the 127th T.M.Battery will relieve the 126th T.M.Battery

2. The Battery on completion of relief will proceed to PIGEON WOOD

3. Two guides will be detailed to conduct relieving sections of the 127th T.M.Battery to the front lines. These guides to be at these Hqrs at 6-50 p.m.
A further guide will be detailed to remain with the 127 T.M.B. for the night of the 4/5th inst to conduct ration parties of the relieving battery to the forward gun positions.

4. All guns complete, handcarts, trench mats + stores will be handed over + receipts obtained.

Sgd. H.J. HAMPSON Capt
O C 126 T.M.Battery.

3/01/18

Battery Operation Order No 36.

1. On the night of the 6/7th inst the 185th M.I.B. will relieve this battery in PIGEON WOOD
2. On completion of relief the battery will proceed to SOUASTRE.
3. Only Trench Maps will be handed over.
4. On completion of relief the battery will proceed by the track leading from the FONQUEVILLERS - ESSARTS ROAD to the HANNESCAMP - ESSARTS ROAD through HANNESCAMP and BIENVILLERS to SOUASTRE.
5. Billets have been arranged at SOUASTRE.

Sgd. H.T HARRISON Capt.
OC 186 Trench battery.

6/4/18

Battery Operation Order No 37.

1) The 186th Inf Bde (less R.W.K. Regt) will move today 7th inst from SOUASTRE

2) The 176th L.T.M.B. will move to HENU.

3) The Battery will parade at 4 open & pass the starting point at the Cross roads, 100 yds E of WINDMILL on SOUASTRE-HENU Road at 4.26 pm.

4) Transport. 1 GS Waggon will be available for transport of gun stores.

     Signed. H.J. HAMPSON Capt

7/4/18   OC 176 L.T.M.Battery.

Battery Operation Order No 38.

1) The 126th H/Bde is relieving the 63rd H/Bde in the line on the night of the 15th inst.
2) This Battery will relieve the 63rd TMB
3) Hqrs will be at F.28.d central
4) All maps, defence schemes etc. will be taken over.
5) The 126th S.I. Pro Hqrs will be at F.28.d.4.6. on and after 9 pm 15th inst.
6) Road will be via SAULCORT and FOUQUEVILLERS.
7) Guides from the 63rd TMB will meet this Battery at FONQUEVILLERS CHURCH at 6.3 pm on the 15th inst.
8) Personnel of Battery, Rear Hqrs & gun teams for the front line will be on her attack stables
9) 1 NCO & 2 men from each of the other 4 gun teams for use as the Second relief for the line.

Sgd. H.J. HAMPSON Capt
15/4/18   O.C. 126 TrenchMortarBattery

Administrative Instructions issued with
Battery Operation Order No 38.

1. Supplies Railhead – SAULTY.
Refilling point on the COUIN-POS ROAD.
2. Water/rations. Water to be brought
up in petrol tins with rations the
same number to be used as the Brigade.
From Battery Hqrs rations will be
carried overland to the gun teams.
3. Trench tramway is available for the
most of the way to the front line
for carrying ammunition.
4. Quartermasters Stores is situated in
the COIGNEAUX area.
5. Trench Tool Depot has been
established at RITTINOY FARM
6. D.A.D.O.S. will be at COUIN.
7. Baths are available at COUIN and
a small tub bath at FONQUEVILLERS.
8. Transport. 1 N. limber will report at
4.30 pm to carry stores required for
the line. 1 S. Waggon will report
at 3. pm to remove stores and
near Hqrs to COIGNEAUX
9. Guns less spare parts will be handed
over at HENU to a representative of the
63rd MGB and receipt obtained.
10. Ammunition will also be handed over
to the 63rd MGB.

11. Only one bicycle will be taken to
Battery Hqrs. Handcarts will not be
taken

              Sgd. H. HAMPSON Capt.
15/4/18   OC 1/16 CMB.

Battery Operation Order no 39.

1. <u>Relief</u>:- A relief of the gun teams in the line, as per attached table, will take place tonight the 18th inst.

2. <u>Rations</u>. Rations will be taken for the 19th inst.

On completion of relief the relieved section will return to Battery Hqrs.

18/4/18.

SIGNED H J HAMPSON
Capt
OC Relic

Relief table in accordance with
Battery O.O. No 39

Section Hqrs.
   Lt H.J. Baldwin relieves Lt Ainsworth
     Servant   "   Servant
     Pte Fitton (R)   "   Pte Dollman (R)

No 1 Gun
   Cpl Sweetman   "   Cpl Keightley
   Pte Thompson   "   Pte Moss
    — Birtwistle   "   — Kavanagh

No 2 Gun
   Cpl Power   "   L/Cpl Gill
   Pte Hall   "   Pte Pease
    — Smith   "   — Robinson

No 3 Gun
   Cpl Stockton   "   Cpl Weakin
   Pte Harrison   "   Pte Lofthouse
    — Hodgson   "   — Harrison

No 4 Gun
   Pte Robertson   "   L/Cpl Johnson
    — Woodward   "   Pte Kearns
    — Baldwin   "   — Foster

Battery Operation Order No. 40

1. <u>Relief</u>. A relief of the gun teams in the line, as per attached table, will take place tonight the ~~18th~~ 22nd inst.

2. <u>Rations</u>. Rations will be taken for the 23rd inst.

On completion of relief, the relieved section will return to Battery Hqrs.

22/1/18.   Signed H J HAMPSON
                                     Capt
                                     OC Relic

Relief table in accordance with
Battery O.O. No 40

Section Hqrs.
Lieut E.O. Morris   relieves   Lieut W.J. Baldwin
Pte Chadwick   —   Pte Sandford
  — Briggs (R)   —   — Fitton (R)

No 1 gun
Cpl Keightley   —   Cpl Sweetman
Pte Jackson   —   Pte Thompson
  — Shaw   —   — Birtwistle

No 2 gun
L/Cpl Jones   —   Cpl Power
Pte Tattersall   —   Pte Hall
  — Proctor   —   — Smith

No 3 gun
Cpl Meakin   —   Cpl Stockton
Pte Hassey   —   Pte Harrison B
  — Holt   —   — Hodgson

No 4 gun
L/Cpl Johnson   —   Pte Robertson
Pte Houghton   —   — Woodward
  — Lennon   —   — Baldwin

Battery Operation Order No 41

1. On the night of the 26/27th inst an intersection relief will take place in accordance with attached table.

2. On the night of the 25th 2 guns will be placed in position in SALMON TRENCH. These 2 guns are to assist in the defence of the strong post SALMON POINT if occasion arises. Positions have been chosen.

3. The amount of ammunition to be made up to 200 rounds per gun

4. Lieut Morris will detail Cpl Meakin to remain in charge of these 2 guns, and supervise construction of the emplacements.

5. On the night of the 25th, a working party will report at 8.0pm to Cpl Meakin at the junction of HIGH STREET and SALMON TRENCH taking spades & sandbags, also the 2 guns & camouflage.
A truck may be used for this purpose.

6. These 2 guns will come under control of Section Hqrs from the night of the 25th inst.

25/4/18

Signed H.T HAMPSON
Capt

Relief table in accordance with
Battery O.O. No 41

Section Hqrs
   Lt Ainsworth   relieves   Lt Morris
   Pte Eastwood   Pte Chadwick
    – Dollman   – Briggs

No 1 gun
   L/Cpl Keighley returns to Batt. Hqrs.
   Pte Ross   relieves   Pte Jackson
    – Kavanagh   –   – Shaw

No 2 gun
   Cpl Power   relieves   L/Cpl Jones
   Pte Pease   –   Pte Tattersall
    – Robinson   –   – Proctor

No 3 gun
   Cpl Stockton   –
   Pte Lofthouse   –   Pte Hussey
    – Harrison   –   – Holt

No 4 gun
   L/Cpl Johnson returns to Batt Hqrs
   Pte Manus   relieves   Pte Houghton
    – Foster   – Levine

No 5 & 6 guns.

Cpl Sweetman relieves Cpl Meakin
Pte McAleese) To proceed as part of the
– Birtwistle) working party on the
– Thompson) night of the 25th equipped
& rationed & to remain
as the gun crews for these
two guns.

25/4/18.

Signed H J HAMPSON
Capt
R.Relic

Battery Operation Order No 42.

1. A relief in accordance with attached table will take place on the night 30th/1st inst.

2. On completion of relief the relieved section will return to Battery Hqrs.

3. Rations will be arranged.

30/4/18.

Signed H J HAMPSON
Capt
OC Relie

Relief table in accordance with
Battery OO No #2

Sect. Hqrs
   Lt Baldwin   relieves   Lt Ainsworth
   Pte Sandford   —   Pte Eastwood
   — Briggs (R)   —   — Dollman (R)

No 1 Gun
   Pte Robertson   —   Pte Moss
   — Proctor   —   — Kavanagh

No 2 Gun
   Cpl Weakin   —   Cpl Power
   Pte Smith   —   Pte Passi
   — Holt   —   — Robinson

No 3 Gun
   Cpl Keightley   —   Cpl Stockton
   Pte Harrison B   —   Pte Lofthouse
   — Hodgson   —   — Harrison

No 4 Gun
   L/Cpl Jones   —   Pte Kearns
   Pte Levine   —   — Foster

No 5 & 6 Guns
   Cpl Knowles   —   Cpl Sweetman
   Pte Jackson   —   Pte McAleese
   — Woodward   —   — Birtwistle
   — Tattersall   —   — Thompson

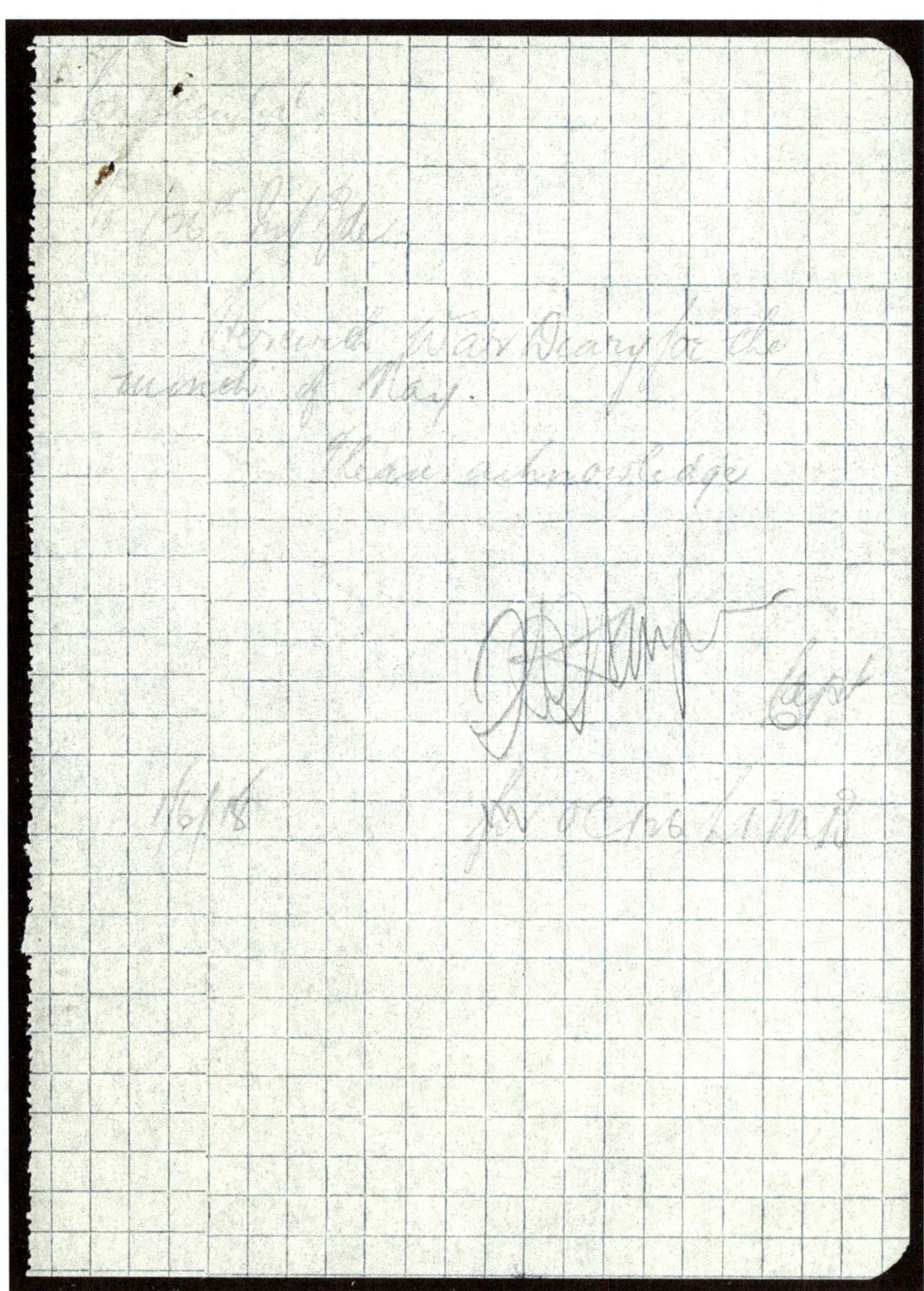

Forwarded War Diary for the
month of May.

Please acknowledge

WAR DIARY
or
INTELLIGENCE SUMMARY.

Army Form C. 2118.

126th Light Trench Mortar Battery

Volume XV

From May 1st 1918 to May 31st 1918.

WAR DIARY or INTELLIGENCE SUMMARY

Army Form C. 2118.

Place	Date	Hour	Summary of Events and Information	Remarks and references to Appendices
LINE Nr. GOMMECOURT WOOD	1/5/18		Hostile M.G's were quiet. A few Granatenwerfer rounds fell in K.6.c.3.8. Our mortars fired 40 rounds into ROSSIGNOL WOOD and on trenches in vicinity. 100 rounds of Stokes ammunition was carried forward at night. Orders received for the relief of the Battery by 125th T.M.B. Battery orders issued for the relief. MOA.	Battery Orders No. 45
"	2/5/18		Hostile T.M's very quiet. About 20 rounds were fired by us at last flying E.A. A fair good effect. Advance party of 3 N.C.O's and 1 runner of the 125th T.M.B. reported 6 April at 2. 30pm. The relieving unit arrived at Batty Hqrs at 7.30pm. Gun teams proceeded to the line. Relief complete at 11. 30pm without casualties. On completion of Relief the Battery moved to billet in BAYENCOURT. The Brigade is Res. Brigade 109th Inf Brigade.	
BAYENCOURT	3/5/18		The men rested during the day. Several cleaning up. A gas guard mounted at Batty Hqrs. MOA	
"	4/5/18		On 10.30am there was a rifle equipment clothing inspection. Football match in the afternoon. MOA	

WAR DIARY or INTELLIGENCE SUMMARY

Army Form C. 2118.

Place	Date	Hour	Summary of Events and Information	Remarks and references to Appendices
BAYENCOURT	5/5/16		Orders received for the relief of the 170th Siege Battery. The Brigade to move to be in Brigade Reserve and to be in the dugouts of the Corps Battery Order issued for the relief of the Battery by the 170th Siege Battery. JDH	Battery Order No 448
"	6/5/16		1 officer from the relieving unit arrived to take over billets etc. The 170th S.R.B. arrived at 3.30pm. On their arrival the Battery proceeded to P.A.S. AREA and took over tents from the 171st S.R.B. 1 Motor lorry placed at the disposal of the Battery for carrying stores to new area. The Battery arrived at its new area at 5.30pm. JDH	
P.A.S. WOODS (C.17.d)	7/5/16		Heavy wet general fatigues. Work commenced on a cookhouse & officers cookhouse. JDH	
"	8/5/16		The Battery paraded at 9am in Brice order for inspection. Work carried on with the erection of cookhouse, orderly room etc.	30/4
"	9/5/16		Orders received for the Brigade to practice Battle the assembling with Battle Positions. The Battery received the order "Practice Battle Positions"	

WAR DIARY
or
INTELLIGENCE SUMMARY

Army Form C. 2118.

Place	Date	Hour	Summary of Events and Information	Remarks and references to Appendices
BATTERSEA PAS WEGES	11/9/18		At 9 a.m. Zero hour. Afternoon(?) at 8 hours. The Battery paraded at 9 a.m. in fighting order marched to assembly position in COLVIN. Orders received to occupy RED LINE. The Battery took up position in the RED LINE. Orders received to march back to billets. Arrived there at 11.30(?) am.	
	12/9/18		The Battery paraded at 9 a.m. Orders received for Inspection of Rifles & Equipment. Remainder of the day spent on fatigues. Work commenced on NCOs mess. OJN	
	13/9/18		Inspection at 9 a.m. Work continued on NCOs mess/Orderly Room. Football in the afternoon. Paid the men of the Battery. OJN	
	14/9/18		1 OR proceeded to the Third Army Rest Camp at SEYMERS. The Battery paraded at 10.15 am for Divine Service. Renewed training in the afternoon. OJN	
	15/9/18		The Battery paraded at 9 a.m. as frozen(?) (as tomorrow?). Work commenced. Horse ran away(?) gun injuring 6 L/Cpl Storey of the 3rd (?) to 1st (?) Base(?) Hospital. OJN	

WAR DIARY
or
INTELLIGENCE SUMMARY.

(Erase heading not required.)

Army Form C. 2118.

Place	Date	Hour	Summary of Events and Information	Remarks and references to Appendices
PAS 11008	14/5/18		Programme of training carried out: course of Physical training, Bayonet drill, Musketry drill, Bayonet & Butt training. Co. parade in morning, Musketry Observance Range lecture in the afternoon. DDM	
"	15/5/18		Daily Programme of training carried out. DDM	
"	16/5/18		The Bn ordered to be prepared at 9 am for training in of personnel to attack the approaches and dealing with MG emplacements by enemy accounts. All NCOs turned at 9 am & proceeded to do recce work for Coy'd schemes. Arranged for the day scheme of Physical, Bayonet, Lewis gun training, Gas Drill, Gas Lecture by Capt. from Lewis Mortar School. Recreational training to take place the evening. DDM	
"	17/5/18		Daily training programme, remainder of Physical, Bayonet & Field training, Musketry, Lewis Drill carried out. DDM	
"	19/5/18		Kit fitting parade at 10 am for Drummer Singer. Recreational training in the afternoon. DDM	

Army Form C. 2118.

WAR DIARY
or
INTELLIGENCE SUMMARY.
(Erase heading not required.)

Instructions regarding War Diaries and Intelligence Summaries are contained in F. S. Regs., Part II. and the Staff Manual respectively. Title pages will be prepared in manuscript.

Place	Date	Hour	Summary of Events and Information	Remarks and references to Appendices
MS WOODS	21/5/16		The Battery paraded at 9 a.m. & proceeded to the RED LINE for work on ammunition & gun emplacements. ADN	
"	22/5/16		The Battery paraded at 9 a.m. & proceeded to the RED LINE and continued work on the area of a task of Self Propelled Gun Emplacements & the area where the new 1.O.R. possible storage for cable and repair (Range Finders) men were moved. ADN	
"	23/5/16		Rain for the day cancelled Musketry Range Practice at arrange ADN free payment of Musket parade. 1.O.R. proceeded to the Hay trying blind of Cutting for a ravine ADN	
"	24/5/16		Daily training Programme carried out. QN	
"	25/5/16		The Battery paraded at 9 a.m. proceeded to the RED LINE for work on ammunition recesses. QN	
"	26/5/16		Daily training Programme carried out. Hygiene Report by Battn M.O. Musketry (Range Practice) Lewis Drill. QN	

WAR DIARY or INTELLIGENCE SUMMARY.

Army Form C. 2118.

(Erase heading not required.)

Place	Date	Hour	Summary of Events and Information	Remarks and references to Appendices
PM Woods	26/5/18		The Battery paraded at 9 a.m. for ceremonial parade. The presentation of Medal Ribbons by the Divisional Commander took place. 6 O.R.'s of the Bn. received ribbons. The Battery paraded at noon for a lecture & sanitation. Remainder training in the afternoon. OBM	
"	27/5/18		Programme of training for the day consisted of drawing Rations in the morning. Musketry, Map reading lecture, Revolver firing in the afternoon. 1 O.R. proceeded to the 3rd Army Rest Camp. OBM	
"	28/5/18		Training in France consisted of Physical Training, Bayonet Fighting in the morning. Ceremonial Drill, Musketry, Recreational Games. 3 O.R. joined the Battery for duty & proceeded from the 3rd Army Rest Camp. OBM 1 taken as attached strength. 1 O.R. proceeded for "Instructional Course" French Mortars in defence.	
"	29/5/18		The Battery paraded at 9 a.m. for instructional lecture "French Mortars in attack." The men had tea at 4.30 p.m. Remainder carried out attack. at 7.30 pm. 1. O.R. joined the Battery for duty & taken on the attached strength. 2. O.R. admitted to hospital sick. OBM	
"	30/5/18		The Battery paraded at 9 a.m. for tactical scheme "French Mortars in attack" & defence.	

Army Form C. 2118.

WAR DIARY
or
INTELLIGENCE SUMMARY.
(Erase heading not required.)

Place	Date	Hour	Summary of Events and Information	Remarks and references to Appendices
PNS WOODS	2/9/18		Musketry & Recreational training in the afternoon. Gas Drill from 9.30pm	
		6.10 a/m	1.OR admitted to Ambulance. NYD	
"	3/9/18		The Battalion paraded at 7.30 am for Initial scheme in co-operation with the 1/6 & 1/7 Manchester Regt. In the afternoon Dummy firing was carried out - (Demonstration) To the rear of the factory at night. Gas Drill from 9.30pm to 10.9pm	

A.Taylor Lieut Col
C.O. 1/6 Lancs

Battery Operation Order No 43

1. The 125th L.T.M. Bty will relieve this Battery on the night of the 2/3 inst.

2. All guns including base plates less spare parts and cleaning rods will be handed over.

3. Maps, Defence Schemes, Trench Stores etc, will be taken over by the relieving Unit & receipts obtained.

4. At 1.30pm on the 2nd inst, a guide will be detailed to meet advance party of 3 NCOs & 1 runner of the 125 L.T.M Bty at the junction of the Mule track and the FONQUEVILLERS - GOMMECOURT Road.

5. A guide will meet Section Hqrs and gun teams of incoming Battery at 4pm at the same place. A further guide will be required at the above place at 8.0pm to conduct Battery Hqrs & remainder of incoming Battery to these Hqrs.

6. Section Hqrs & gun teams when relieved will proceed direct to BAYENCOURT via CHATEAU de la HAID. A guide will meet them at the Church in BAYENCOURT.

7. Lieut Baldwin will detail a man to report to these present Hqrs relief complete.

8. C/R Stockton & 2 men will proceed and report to the Hqrs of 125 XTM Bty in BAYENCOURT to take over billets by 10am on the 2nd inst.

9. Rear Hqrs will endeavour to arrange hot tea on the Battery's arrival at BAYENCOURT. Time of arrival 11 pm.

10. Rear Hqrs will note that no gun boxes are to be handed over.

11. Transport. Orders will be issued later, but a limber will be available.

12. All surplus stores etc must be returned by ration limber tonight.

13. Dug outs, latrines etc must be handed over in a sanitary condition.

1/5/18.

Signed H J HAMPSON
Capt
OC Relief

Battery Operations Order No. 44

Ref 55° 40000

1. The 126th L.T.M Battery will be relieved by the 170th T.M. Battery and take over billets of the 171st T.M. Battery at C 22 d 3 1 on the 6th inst.

2. 2/Lt Morris and 2 OR at present at P.18 will act as advance party and take over billets etc.

3. The Battery will move off on arrival of relieving unit at 3 p.m.

4. Transport available will be notified later.

5. Brigade HQrs will re-open at C 16 d 3b 15.

(Signed) H.J. HAMPSON. Capt.

2/5/18

O.C. 126 L.T.M Battery

...

(Signed) H Harrison Lt.Col.
3/5/18   OC 176 L.W. Coy

Army Form C. 2118.

CONFIDENTIAL

WAR DIARY
or
INTELLIGENCE SUMMARY.
(Erase heading not required.)

126th Light Trench Mortar Battery.

Volume XVI.

From June 1st 1918 to June 30th 1918.

Place	Date	Hour	Summary of Events and Information	Remarks and references to Appendices

WAR DIARY
INTELLIGENCE SUMMARY
(Erase heading not required.)

Army Form C. 2118.

Place	Date	Hour	Summary of Events and Information	Remarks and references to Appendices
OIS WOODS (Sqd 33)	1/6/18		Training for the morning consisted of drivering drill. Half holiday in the afternoon.	
"	2/6/18	10am	Divine Service. Pte May returned to Brigade Hqrs. 1 OR rejoined the Battery from hospital. 1 OR joined the Battery for duty and taken on the strength. strength of 1 OR. The Battery furnished at 10 a.m. for Divine Service. JM	
"	3/6/18		Training programme for the day consisted of Physical & Bayonet Training. Lecture by Lieut. Mackley, Musketry & practical proceedings of the 1/63 Lgt H Bgn by the Observation Officer received for the relief of the 1/63 Lgt Bgn by the 1/62 Lgt Bgde. 1 OR proceeded on 14 days special leave. JM	
"	4/6/18		Training for the day consisted of Physical & Bayonet training, Musketry (Range practice). Signed Honourable Order Received. Musketry of JM	
"	5/6/18		Training programme consisted of Physical & Bayonet Training. Lectures. Supplies were taken to various places. JM	
"	6/6/18		Afternoon parties proceeded to the lines.	Battery Orders

WAR DIARY

INTELLIGENCE SUMMARY.

(Erase heading not required.)

Army Form C. 2118.

Place	Date	Hour	Summary of Events and Information	Remarks and references to Appendices
PNS WOODS (C.17.A.3.2) and	7/6/18		The Battery paraded at 12. 30pm and proceeded to the line to relieve the 7th M.N. T.M. Battery	
T.2 and 66.38 Battery Hqrs			Relief completed by 5.30pm. The Nucleus & personnel of Rear Hqrs moved to LOUVENCOURT.	
LINE Battery Hqrs 5.2.H. at 66.39.	8/6/18		During our bombardment on the Right of the Divisional Enemy T.Ms were slightly active on Right Battalion front. 60 rounds were fired by our mortars on various targets which carried out cleaning ammunition test.	
"	9/6/18		Mobile T.M.s were very quiet. 40 rounds were fired clearing the ammunition by our mortars. Enemy fired at K.30.c 25.90 which was observed to be enemy mortar fired on with good effect. I don't think enemy observed. 15th crossed on with sanitary ammunition. T.M. proceeded to the Rear Hqrs Rest Camp.	
"	10/6/18		Enemy Mortars slightly active. Our mortars fired 75 rounds on various targets including LA SIGNY FARM. T.M. fired fired our own lines about 6pm. 10 rounds were fired and the E.A. fired back toward to our line.	

WAR DIARY / INTELLIGENCE SUMMARY

Army Form C. 2118.

Place	Date	Hour	Summary of Events and Information	Remarks and references to Appendices
LINE Batty Hqrs Fort 2 K.6.30	11/6/18		Enemy T.M's fired a few rounds onto K.33.A.80.30. Trenches were fired by our Mortars during the day. O.P to Open at 101 feet. OISEU FARM was fired over. Heavily shelled about 6p.m. to 6.30. pm. Hot gun and Howitzer emplacement at K.33.d.80.40. and at Quinconce in Trenches. An accurate T.M. emplacement K.33 was covered by machine gun fire. Enemy T.M's very quiet. Our Mortars fired 25 rounds in every the day. Ice water active when rifle's carried out in the afternoon.	
"	12/6/18		Mobile T.M's active against French Junction 200 K.33.b.85.15. Our mortars fires 50 rounds on Bosed Wood and a dugout at K.33.a.60.40. During the evening an spd burst on K.20 SIGNY FARM (to the craters) on M.G emplacement of Hot gun emplacement of K.33.d.50.40 and enjoying annoyances 1 or moved by the two Trench Mortar (Battery) O.P.	
"	13/6/18		Enemy T.M's more active. The enemy shewed an almost direct hit	

WAR DIARY
INTELLIGENCE SUMMARY

Army Form C. 2118.

(Erase heading not required.)

Instructions regarding War Diaries and Intelligence Summaries are contained in F.S. Regs., Part II. and the Staff Manual respectively. Title pages will be prepared in manuscript.

Place	Date	Hour	Summary of Events and Information	Remarks and references to Appendices
LINE Sector Hgn Toudos 36	15/6/18		On our No 2 gun destroying most of the ammunition. 75 rounds were fired by our mortars chiefly in retaliation on to K31a 35. 70 and L25 (SIGNY FARM). Work done on emplacement at K33 d 60 just partly destroyed) 1 OR report from 2nd Army School of Cookery. NDN Fairly quiet. Enemy mortars fired 200 rounds during the day. The targets being VALHOF TRENCH and Sunday Road at K33b 80 20 K31a6 K29d 85 10, K27.17.9 and) LA SIGNY FARM. Work carried on with No 1 emplacement and carrying ammunition & salvage. Relief carried out, of No 2 gun Battery detachment in the line. NDN	Battery Order No 47
	16/6/18		Enemy TMs very quiet. Our Mortars fired 60 rounds during the day & night. The chief target being the wire in front of WATLING ST in K34C. Work carried on with no new dug out on No 1 gun. Carrying ammunition & salvage. Orders issued for inter- section relief. NDN	Battery Order No 48

WAR DIARY
INTELLIGENCE SUMMARY

Army Form C. 2118.

Place	Date	Hour	Summary of Events and Information	Remarks and references to Appendices
LINE Battery Posn T31d.66.38	17/6/18		Hostile TMs fairly quiet. 60 rounds were fired by our Mortars during the day & night. The were in front of WYOMING ST (N3nd) was again fired on. They dug out in SIXTH AVENUE (N33d 50.55) completed. An inter-aviation strafe was carried out in the afternoon. 1 O.R. returned from leave. MM	
"	18/6/18		Battery 70 rounds issued. Enemy TMs very quiet during the day. A 2 minute barrage was put up on to MARTIN'S ST in N31c & N31a in support of a raid. 300 rounds were expended. Work carried on constructing emplacement for the raid & carrying ammunition. MM	Battery Gns 116.9
"	19/6/18		Enemy TMs very quiet, a few Minenwerfer bombs being fired on Left Battalion front at N27b. 50 rounds were fired by our Mortars in retaliation on to LA SIGNY FARM and trenches in N27d. Direct hits being obtained. Ammunition was carried up to the forward area. Battery O.O. No 50 issued. 3 O.R. proceeded to the Div. Convalescent Camp for 10 days. MM	Battery Gns 116.55

WAR DIARY
INTELLIGENCE SUMMARY
(Erase heading not required.)

Army Form C. 2118.

Place	Date	Hour	Summary of Events and Information	Remarks and references to Appendices
LINE Battery Hqrs T24d 66.38	20/6/16		Enemy TMs quiet. 250 rounds were fired by our Mortars during the day and night chiefly in support of the daylight raid on post at K34d 19.34. A barrage was put round the post and cased on a prearranged signal of one red verey light. After rounds were also fired on trenches in K27d and the track leading to LA SIGNY FARM. Ammunition was carried up to forward dug. Any intersector relief was carried out during the afternoon. JN	Battery Orders No 51
	21/6/16		Enemy TMs showed slight activity about 20 rounds being fired on our front line system about K34c 30.70 by enemy Minenwerfer 45 rounds were fired in retaliation on to K34a 75.40 where the Minenwerfer appeared to be firing from. After the first few rounds the hostile Mortars ceased fire. A further 40 rounds were fired in retaliation to enemy artillery shelling our front line the targets being LA SIGNY FARM and enemy post K27d 7.9 Ammunition was carried up to forward area. Battery O.O. No 51 issued. JN	Battery Orders No 51

WAR DIARY / INTELLIGENCE SUMMARY

Army Form C. 2118.

Place	Date	Hour	Summary of Events and Information	Remarks and references to Appendices
LINE BATTERY H&RS J2.d.6.38	22/6/18		Enemy TMs quiet. 53 rounds were fired by our Mortars during the daylight night on to targets K27d and VALLADE TRENCH (K3 central). Work carried on enlarging ammunition MN.	
	23/6/18		The Battery was relieved by the 127th T.M. Battery. On completion of relief the Battery moved to BUS WOODS and took over the Camp vacated by the 127 T.M. B.y. 1 O.R. proceeded to Third Army Rest Camp. 1 O.R. returned from Third Army Rest Camp. MN	
BUS WOODS	24/6/18		Battery paraded at 8.0 am for baths. On return to camp work was carried on improving bivouacs etc. Recreational training in the afternoon. 1 O.R. proceeded on 14 days leave to UK. 4 O.R.s returned to Units. Cpl Keightley awarded the Meritorious Service Medal. ODN	
	25/6/18		Battery paraded at 9.0 am for Rifle Inspection & general fatigues. Recreational training in the afternoon. ODN	
	26/6/18		Battery paraded at 9.30 am for Rifle Gas Helmet and Kit Inspection. Games & Recreational training in the afternoon.	

Army Form C. 2118.

WAR DIARY
or
INTELLIGENCE SUMMARY
(Erase heading not required.)

Place	Date	Hour	Summary of Events and Information	Remarks and references to Appendices
BUS WOODS	27/6/18		Battery paraded at 9.30 am in Battle Order for inspection of Rifles & Equipment, and at 10.0 am for cleaning guns & inspection. Recreational training in the afternoon. MM	
	28/6/18		Battery paraded at 9.30 am for inspection. Games & recreational training in the afternoon. MM	
	29/6/18		Parade during the morning consisted of Physical training and Bayonet fighting, Musketry and Gas Drill. Recreational training in the afternoon. 1 OR proceeded on 14 days leave to UK. Operation Orders received for relief. MM	
	30/6/18		Battery paraded for Divine Service at 9.30 am. MM	

M. Hampsen. Capt.
O.C. 131st Battery

126th Light Trench Mortar Battery

War Diary

Volume XVII

From 1st July 1918 to 31st July 1918

WAR DIARY
INTELLIGENCE SUMMARY
(Erase heading not required.)

Army Form C. 2118.

Place	Date	Hour	Summary of Events and Information	Remarks and references to Appendices
BUS	1/7/18		A working party consisting of 1 Off. 4 N.C.O. + 27 men paraded in fighting order at 7.15am and reported to H.Qrs. 1/4th Manchester Regt. Remainder of the Battery paraded at 9.30am for Baths at LOUVENCOURT. 1 N.C.O. proceeded to H.Qrs. 125th T.M. Battery to take over T.M. guns. 1 N.C.O. granted 10 days leave to PARIS. Battery Operation Orders issued for the move into the Line. OW	Battery Notes No. 1–2.
"	2/7/18		The Battery paraded at 1.30pm and marched to new Hqrs at K.25.d.0.5. One gun of the 127 T.M. Battery was taken over at K.15.d. 20.25. and one gun of placed in position at K.15.d. 35.20. Nucleus & Rear Hqrs. moved from BUS to LOUVENCOURT. OW	
LINE Battery Hqrs K.25.d.0.5	3/7/18		Enemy T.M. quiet. Our Mortars fired burst at intervals on to CETADRIX and GUESCAIN Trenches in K.22.a. 30 rounds were expended. Work commenced on emplacements at K.27.a.50.10. and K.27.a.50.85. OW	

Army Form C. 2118.

WAR DIARY or INTELLIGENCE SUMMARY.
(Erase heading not required.)

Place	Date	Hour	Summary of Events and Information	Remarks and references to Appendices
LINE. Fatty Alps (A3518.a.51)	4/9/16		Enemy T.M. quiet. Rapid bursts were again fired by our mortars at varying intervals on L. CETORIX and L. GUESCHIN trenches. No troops were observed. 2.1 O.P. guns were placed in position at K.27.a.50.80, K.27.a.50.85 and ammunition carried to these guns.	
"	5/9/16		Bursts 6 were fired during day and night on L. GUESCHIN, JENA, and CETORIX trenches, and traversing along CETORIX trenches in K.22.a. No 1b gun at K.22.a.30.55 also fired on. 80 rounds were expended. During our firing enemy sent up whistle very light which were followed by slight retaliation from 77mm guns. Work carried out on improvement of gun emplacements & dug out at Fee Alps. Battery orders issued for occupation relief.	Battery Order No. 52.
"	6/9/16		Enemy T.M. inactive. CETORIX and JENA trenches were again fired on by our mortars. Short raft bursts were also fired on to the junction of Mere G trench. No troops were observed. Work carried on with emplacements & dug outs dug out.	Battery Order No. 53.

WAR DIARY / INTELLIGENCE SUMMARY

Army Form C. 2118.

Place	Date	Hour	Summary of Events and Information	Remarks and references to Appendices
LINE Bully Hyn K.28.b.8.5.	17/7/18		Enemy T.M. quiet. Our mortars fired 50 rounds during the day, the targets being CICORIA AVENUE, JENTA and PALESTINE AVENUE, also fired at K.28.a.1.9. Work carried on with emplacement in FORT STEWART. 1 O.R. proceeded to the 43rd Heavy Field Amb. 1 O.R. reported from the Rest Camp and 1 O.R. reported from the 43rd Heavy Field of Bakery. JW	
	18/7/18		Between 2 am and 2.30 am enemy fired yellow cross gas shells into areas K.19, K.25, K.26c, K.31 and K.32 (being to the concentration of gas in K.25. Bakery Hqrs were evacuated and moved to T.2.c.9.8. Our mortars fired 98 rounds on to Zench function K.28.a.t.6 and enemy front line K.28.a.0.8. Men worked on carrying ammunition to Stokes emplacements. JW	
Jerking Hqr 17/7/18 T.2.c.g.8.	19/7/18		Enemy T.M's on the Brigade Front were very quiet. Between 12 hrs and 2 and our mortars fired 50 rounds on to strafers in SUNKEN ROAD (K.22.a.) also enemy post at K.28.a.10.60. Lews guns were fired extensively in FORT STEWART. JW	

Army Form C. 2118.

4

WAR DIARY
or
INTELLIGENCE SUMMARY.

(Erase heading not required.)

Instructions regarding War Diaries and Intelligence Summaries are contained in F. S. Regs., Part II. and the Staff Manual respectively. Title pages will be prepared in manuscript.

Place	Date	Hour	Summary of Events and Information	Remarks and references to Appendices
Jabeeq Aps T.20.d.9.8.	10/7/18		Enemy T.M. very quiet. Fifteen Whizz bang short bursts on/over (?) by own mortars on to trench in K.28.a.02.90 and K.28.a.05.70. 40 rounds were expended. Work carried on with emplacements in FORT STEWART. 9H.	
"	11/7/18		Enemy T.M. quiet. Our mortars fired 80 rounds in short bursts on K.22.a.40.60 and K.28.a.90.10. direct hits being obtained. 9H	
"	12/7/18		Enemy T.M. quiet. Our mortars fired 120 rounds on to trench junctions on K.22.a. SUNKEN ROAD (K.22.a.22.50.) and trench at K.28.a.10.90. Short bursts were fired during night on positions reported at K.22.c.33.75. Work carried out improving emplacements in FORT STEWART and accessory ammunition. 9H	
"	13/7/18		Our mortars fired 185 rounds during day and night. At 11am and 7pm shoots were carried out in co-operation with Medium T.M on CESTRIX AVENUE, GYESCEIN TRENCH reported job and trench junctions in K.22.c. Several direct hits were observed. During the night harassing fire on short bursts was maintained on the above targets and the	

A5834 Wt.W4973/M687 750,000 8/16 D. D. & L. Ltd. Forms/C.2118/13.

Army Form C. 2118.

WAR DIARY
or
INTELLIGENCE SUMMARY.
(Erase heading not required.)

Place	Date	Hour	Summary of Events and Information	Remarks and references to Appendices
Battery Posn K.29.c.9.			Addition to MARCH 31 (FORT SUSEX) and enemy front line near K.22.0 The enemy retaliated slightly with M.G. arms on the southern edge of HEBUTERNE. Work done towards digging new emplacement to at K.19.c.It.9.5. and on two accounts to in FORT SUSEX. Battery Orders issued for temporary setup.	Battery Orders Sent
"	1/4/16		Enemy T.M. against our front line mortars fired 55 rounds on trenches in K.21a 2 four gun wire entrenchments from K.20 K.35 and placed in the strong points locality K.19c. K.20.	
"	2/4/16		Enemy T.M. (F.O.) an occasional shot on K.27.b.0.1. Our mortars fired 35 rounds on H, enemy forward posts in K.26 and K.27. No reports the Battery from leave.	
"	3/4/16		Enemy T.M. quiet. 60 rounds were fired by our mortars during the day enemy front line K.28.a.05.40. 06.60.70 and K.27.6.95.85 on enemy front line of line to the lower target one of the enemy was at 1.1.15pm averaged a burst on the trench. Obs. I have one of	

Army Form C. 2118.

WAR DIARY
or
INTELLIGENCE SUMMARY.
(Erase heading not required.)

Instructions regarding War Diaries and Intelligence Summaries are contained in F. S. Regs., Part II. and the Staff Manual respectively. Title pages will be prepared in manuscript.

Place	Date	Hour	Summary of Events and Information	Remarks and references to Appendices
Factory/Agre T.19.c.40.15.	17/7/18		Our Trench Mortars fired at a place thought attended to cross our lines. Enemy Mgrs active from T.20.c.9.5 to T.19.c.40.15. JM. Enemy TM guns shot 3 rds short [?] rds far and on to enemy front line K.28.a.0.40, K.26.a.0.60, K.26.a.00.70 and K.29.b.90.65. Stretchers were expended. 1 OR admitted Fd. Ambulance. 3 ORs Relief No.99 received. Relief orders issued for the relief JM.	Enemy report JM
"	18/7/18		Some Rear Mgr and Fwd Lovencourt to Bus Wood. Fire [?] on enemy MG Post (Ref. unknown) to Bus Wood and took over the camp vacated by 127 [Infantry] Battalion. 3 OR admitted Fd. Ambulance. JM	
BUS WOOD	19/7/18		Men rested during the day. Returned clothes to the men 1 pr. each P. 30 pm to 9 pm JM.	
"	20/7/18		Gen [Eclipse] General cleaning up. LOR proceeded England [on leave] to Wales as [?] Mortar Instructor (Auth 30/Adj.4.00 FS/R.G.W./8-24/5/0) Nil Mt/Macklean arr. admitted Fd Amb Fract Skull. 2 OR admitted Fd. Amb. 1 sick. JM	
"	21/7/18		Voluntary Church Parade.	

WAR DIARY
INTELLIGENCE SUMMARY
(Erase heading not required.)

Army Form C. 2118.

Place	Date	Hour	Summary of Events and Information	Remarks and references to Appendices
BUS WOOD	22/7/16		The Battery paraded at 9.30am for Kit Inspection followed by medical inspection at 10. Educational Training. 2 OR named to attend a 2 OR course at Artillery School of Instruction, reported to Battery for duties from 12 N. 22/7/16	
"	23/7/16		Battery paraded for Rifle Inspection, musketry Lecture & Physical training. 3 OR were on the strength of the Battery to complete establishment. 3 OR advanced field truck. 200 N	
	24/7/16		1 OR admitted field truck. 1 OR reported from hospital. Admin. received for the relief of the 126th By by the 98th By.	
	25/7/16		Working party proceeded at 6.30am for digging emplacements. Admin. order received for the relief of the 98th Bdr. by the 67th Bdr. Battery to commence for the relief & to proceed to gun pits 200 N	
	26/7/16		Advance party proceeded to new Battery Hqrs to take over. The Battery paraded	

WAR DIARY or INTELLIGENCE SUMMARY.

Army Form C. 2118.

Place	Date	Hour	Summary of Events and Information	Remarks and references to Appendices
Battery Hqrs. S.a.70.70	26/9/18		For rifle inspection at 9.30am. Several fatigues cleaning camp. The Battery paraded at 2.30 pm. marched to the line. Rear Hqrs arrived moved to VOUVERCOURT. JN	
"	27/9/18		Enemy M.G's very quiet. Work carried on with entrenchment and drainage of gun pits cleaning ammunition. JN	
"	28/9/18		Enemy M.G's moderate. Heavy gas shelling took place between 1am & 2.30am about K.31 and K.32. New S.O.S position for No.3 gun commenced at K.27.c.85.75. Capt. N.J. Hampton M.C. rejoined the Battery from convalescent camp. JN	
"	29/9/18		Enemy M.G's very quiet. A large number of gas shells fell on the Brigade area during the night. Work carried on with new S.O.S position for No 3 gun. 2 new ammunition recesses built at 6 & 7 gun positions. New S.O.S Ammunition overhauled & cleaned. Battery Orders issued for intersection relief. JN	Battery Orders No. S.9
"	30/9/18		Enemy M.G's moderate. Work carried on with new S.O.S position for No.3 gun. JN	

Army Form C. 2118.

WAR DIARY
or
INTELLIGENCE SUMMARY.
(Erase heading not required.)

Instructions regarding War Diaries and Intelligence Summaries are contained in F. S. Regs., Part II and the Staff Manual respectively. Title pages will be prepared in manuscript.

Place	Date	Hour	Summary of Events and Information	Remarks and references to Appendices
FORT BERTHM P.S.A.70.90	3/9/18		Enemy M.G. very quiet. Work continues on new headers for 1/2 3 guns. 2 ad't reported the Battery from 23rd Divl. Amm. Column 9/9/18	

M. Mark Capt.
O.C. 116. L.T.M. Battery.

Army Form C. 2118.

126 L.T.M. Battery

WAR DIARY
or
INTELLIGENCE SUMMARY.
(Erase heading not required.)

Place	Date	Hour	Summary of Events and Information	Remarks and references to Appendices
FORT BEAUMONT	1/8/18		Enemy T.M's very quiet. Offensive positions prepared near CHEEROH AVENUE and NEWGATE STR. 240 rounds of ammunition taken up to forward dump. The next T.M.I position for the 3 gun completed. DAN	
"	2/9/18		Enemy T.M's moderate. Our mortars fired a few rounds as warning shots. N.2 set a 20 rounds. Ammunition were taken up from dump to forward positions in preparation for the new role. DAN	Battery Order No. 58
"	3/9/18		Enemy T.M's very quiet. Stok carried on with assembling and changing ammunition and entrenching tools to forward positions for the relief of No.14 gun team. DAN	
"	4/9/18		No enemy T.M's was traced. Our mortars fired 120 rounds on to WASSING STR. from 1.50 a 2.15 & 2.35 a 2.50. New ammunition reccie'd with for the No.3 gun Battery Orders. DAN	Battery Order No. 59

WAR DIARY
of
INTELLIGENCE SUMMARY.

(Erase heading not required.)

Army Form C. 2118.

Place	Date	Hour	Summary of Events and Information	Remarks and references to Appendices
FORT BERTHA	5/8/18		Hostile TM's very quiet. 250 rounds of stokes ammunition were carried from forward Dumps to gun positions. Test shelters built for No. 3 gun team.	
"	6/8/18		Enemy TM's inactive between 2 & 13 pm our mortars fired 120 rounds on to trench running from 11.3.d a.50.80 to K.31 a.35.30. Work carried on with preparing & carrying ammunition and rebuilding base plate positions.	
"	7/8/18		Enemy TM's very quiet. 250 rounds of stokes ammunition carried from forward Dumps to guns and assembly. 162 rounds disposed the Battery from 117 Res. Brigade I Bank. Orders issued for relief of No. 1 gun team. New mortar fired 120 rounds on to enemy wire from K.31 a.20.90 to K.31 a.75.40. 360 rounds stokes ammunition taken to forward dumps.	Battery Orders No 60.

WAR DIARY
or
INTELLIGENCE SUMMARY.

(Erase heading not required.)

Army Form C. 2118.

Place	Date	Hour	Summary of Events and Information	Remarks and references to Appendices
FORT BERTHA	8/1/18		10.10 GHR. Very quiet. Our mortars fired 200 rounds on enemy wire from K.35.a.3.75 to K.35.c.3.0 and 30 rounds to breach our GREEN S.TR and TRACKS.	
"	9/1/18		Our mortars fired 30 rounds on GREEN TR and the TRIANGLE. Registration was carried out on BOCHE WOOD and N horn of GREEN TR. Work carried on preparing defences for our counter attack organized in conjunction with the attack by the 9th Brigade on Factory line. Battery Orders issued in hypothesis of K.35.a, C.ed. 30th W/O Maude to hip our enemy Trench system at K.35.a, C.ed. 30th	Battery Order No. 61
"	10/1/18		An attack [undone?] to endeavour to establish conditions. Enemy MG's unusual. Our mortars fired 30 rounds on GREEN TR. VILLAGE TR and the RESERVE. Work carries on preparing ammunition.	
"	11/1/18		Orders received for the relief of the Battery by 129th R.F.A. The Battery on completion of relief moves to BUS WOOD and takes over the emplacements by 127 Army F. Bar. Hy's Stores moved from LOUVENCOURT to BUS WOODS.	Battery Order No. 62

Army Form C. 2118.

WAR DIARY
or
INTELLIGENCE SUMMARY.
(Erase heading not required.)

Instructions regarding War Diaries and Intelligence Summaries are contained in F.S. Regs., Part II. and the Staff Manual respectively. Title pages will be prepared in manuscript.

Place	Date	Hour	Summary of Events and Information	Remarks and references to Appendices
BUS WOODS	13/9/18		Men rested during the day. OR proceeded on leave to U.K. OA	
"	14/9/18		Weather equipment & general fatigues. The fatigue parades for bath at Loyne Hogart at 9.30 am. 2 O.R. proceeded on today's K.E.O. Morris to Hostels. High cost & 1 O.R. proceeded on today's leave to U.K. OA	
"	15/9/18		The fatigue parades for rifle Hit zero inspection. 1 OR proceeded on 10 days leave to U.K. OA	
"	16/9/18		Training for the day consists of Physical training Bayonet fighting Squadrill Musketry. OA	
"	17/9/18		The fatigue parades for Physical training Bayonet fighting Squadrill musketry together together with number of 1 NCO proceeded to the 6/1st School for the next course at stokes Mor. tar school. OA	
"	18/9/18		Voluntary Church parades in the morning. Recruitment training in the afternoon. OA	

WAR DIARY
or
INTELLIGENCE SUMMARY.
(Erase heading not required.)

Army Form C. 2118.

Place	Date	Hour	Summary of Events and Information	Remarks and references to Appendices
BUS WOOD	19/8/18		Programme of training carried out in the morning. General camp fatigues in the afternoon. JGN.	
BERTRANCOURT	20/8/18		Orders received for the Battery to move to BERTRANCOURT. The Battery paraded at 2.0pm and marched to BERTRANCOURT and took over billets. JGN.	
"	21/8/18		The 125th and 127th Inf Brigades attacked in conjunction with the Division on the right and left. The 126th Inf Brigade held in Divisional reserve. Orders received for the Brigade to be ready to move at one hours notice. Battery Wgn closed at BERTRANCOURT and re opened at FORT STEWART (K.20.b.) at 10. p.m. JGN.	
FORT STEWART	22/8/18		Warning Order received for the Brigade to attack IRLES in conjunction with the 37th Div. on the right. Attended conference at Hqrs 126th Inf Bde & considered the method of attack Attack cancelled. The Brigade to hold themselves in readiness to relieve 125th Inf Bde. JGN.	
"	23/8/18		A Baldwin v.g. NCO. recommended the ground in view of relief of 125th Inf B. Battery orders in case of relief Verbal message received for the Battery to relieve the 125th Inf.B. JGN.	Battery Orders No. 67

WAR DIARY
INTELLIGENCE SUMMARY

Army Form C. 2118.

Place	Date	Hour	Summary of Events and Information	Remarks and references to Appendices
FORT STEWART (K.20.f.)	1/8/18		At dawn the Battery relieved the 109th MB. Relief completed at 6.30am.	
			1 OR proceeded on 14 days leave to U.K.	
	2/8/18		Battery HQrs moved from FORT STEWART to SERRE. The Division not in reserve. Orders received for the Battery to move to LEOPARD WOOD AREA. Battery orders issued for the move. HQrs	
	3/8/18		The Battery paraded at 9.30am & marched to new area. HQrs established at LITTLE WOOD.	
LITTLE WOOD (M9.d.9.8.)	27/8/18		Reconnoitred the line & red a new & possible gun emplacement. Front line runs through LA BARQUE.	
	28/8/18		1 gun placed at M.12.6.70.59. Le Gn HQrs at M.12.K.oo.60. 2 guns at M.12.6.70.59 being place tracking THILLOY. HQrs moved to LA BARQUE.	
	29/8/18		Positions reconnoitred near RIENCOURT. Orders received for the 109th A/B.de to relieve the 126th A/Bde. The 109th Btmd relieves the 126th MB.	2 guns at M.12.6.70.65

Army Form C. 2118.

WAR DIARY
INTELLIGENCE SUMMARY.
(Erase heading not required.)

Place	Date	Hour	Summary of Events and Information	Remarks and references to Appendices
LA BARQUE and PYS	31/8/18		Orders received for the 175th L/M Bde to relieve the 176th L/M Bde. The 175th L/M B. relieved the 176th L/M B. On completion of relief the Battery moved to PYS and took over the camp vacated by the 125th L.T.M. Battery.	

M.W.Campbell Capt.
O.C. 175. L.T.M Battery.

126th Light Trench Mortar Battery.

War Diary

Volume XIX

From Sept 1st 1918 to Sept 30th 1918

Army Form C. 2118.

WAR DIARY
or
INTELLIGENCE SUMMARY.
(Erase heading not required.)

Instructions regarding War Diaries and Intelligence Summaries are contained in F.S. Regs., Part II. and the Staff Manual respectively. Title pages will be prepared in manuscript.

Place	Date	Hour	Summary of Events and Information	Remarks and references to Appendices
PYS.	1/9/18		The Brigade in Divisional Reserve. Battery Officers moved across the valley and joined Rear Hqrs. WSV	
	2/9/18		Men rested during the day. WSV	
	3/9/18		The Ladies at WARLENCOURT allotted from 11am to 12 noon. The Battery handed for baths at 10.30 a.m. Orders received for the Battery to move forward under orders of the C.O. 15th Manchester Regt. the reserve battalion. The Battery paraded at 1pm and marched to RIENCOURT. Halted in the vicinity and partook of mid day meal. Afterwards moved forward to VILLERS-AU-FLOS. Cavalry reported beyond YPRES. The Battery remained at VILLERS-AU-FLOS. The 126th Inf. Brigade took in Divisional Reserve. WSV	
	4/9/18		Orders received for the Division to continue the advance, the final objective being the trenches in front of METZ-en-COUTURE. WSV	

Army Form C. 2118.

WAR DIARY
INTELLIGENCE SUMMARY
(Erase heading not required.)

Place	Date	Hour	Summary of Events and Information	Remarks and references to Appendices
VILLERS-AU-FLOS.	5/9/18		Orders received that 126th Division is being relieved by the N.Z. Division on the night 5/6th & that the 126th Div. will march to SAROU area on the morning of the 6th Oct. The 126th Div'l Artillery however at LUISENHOF FARM. 4B/	
	6/9/18		The Battery paraded at 9.30 am & then the starting point at 9.50am, arriving at LUISENHOF FARM at 12.30 pm. 3B/ 4B/	
LUISENHOF FARM.	7/9/18		Men rested during the day. 1 OR admitted 33rd Fd Amb.	
"	8/9/18		Stables, fatigues, General cleaning up & Voluntary church parades. 2L. Dudworth proceeded on 14 days leave to U.K. 3B/ 4B/	
"	9/9/18		Cleaning the camp & belonging material. 4B/ 1 OR rejoined the Battery from labor.	
"	10/9/18		Training for the day consisted of Musketry, Gas Drill & Refresher Lecture. 3B/ 2 OR rejoined from leave.	

Army Form C. 2118.

WAR DIARY
or
INTELLIGENCE SUMMARY.
(Erase heading not required.)

Instructions regarding War Diaries and Intelligence Summaries are contained in F. S. Regs., Part II. and the Staff Manual respectively. Title pages will be prepared in manuscript.

Place	Date	Hour	Summary of Events and Information	Remarks and references to Appendices
LUISENHOF FARM.	11/9/16		Tactical Scheme carried out in conjunction with a company of the 1/4th Manchester Regt.	
"	12/9/16		1 OR rejoined the Battery from leave. 2 OR's rejoined the Battery from hospital.	
"	13/9/16		Training for the day consisted of Musketry (Range practice) Maps & Compass work, & Refresher Lectures.	
"	14/9/16		Tactical Scheme carried out in conjunction with the 1/4 Manchester Regt.	
"	15/9/16		Training for the day consisted of Musketry (Range practice), Lectures. Battery paraded for Divine Service at 9.45 am. 1 OR (wounded) (free) Ambulance.	
"	16/9/16		The Battery paraded at 9 am for Tactical scheme with Dummy Tanks. 1 OR rejoined from leave.	
"	17/9/16		Training for the morning consisted of Musketry, Bayonet fighting, & Bombing. The Bache at TILLOY acted as the Factory from 11 am to 1 noon. In the afternoon	

WAR DIARY or INTELLIGENCE SUMMARY

Army Form C. 2118.

Place	Date	Hour	Summary of Events and Information	Remarks and references to Appendices
LUISENHOF FARM	18/9/18		Consisted of a Lecture Scheme in conjunction with the 1st Manchester Regt. E.B. The Battery paraded for Gen. Brell Maj Lenham leading them Race.	
"	19/9/18		Recreational training in the afternoon. Orders received for the Brigade to stand to. The S.O.S. went up along the Corps Front. The Germans attacked our positions but were repulsed with heavy losses. Orders received to stand down but to be ready to move at 2 minutes notice. E.B. Warning Order received for the 42nd Div. to relieve the 37th Division the line. Operation Administrative Orders received for the Bde to relieve the 111th & 67th Inf. Bdes on the 20th & 21st inst. Battery Orders issued for the relief. E.B.	Battery orders No. 6 & 7
"	20/9/18		1. Motor lorry 12/8 Reserve reported to the Battery for the transport of guns, ammunition, stores to LEBUCQUIERE. The Battery paraded at 10.30 am marched to I.29.K.0.3. and took over the camp vacated by the 111th Bty R.F.A. Move complete by 1.30 pm. W.B.	
I.29.K.0.3.				

Army Form C. 2118.

WAR DIARY
or
INTELLIGENCE SUMMARY.
(Erase heading not required.)

Place	Date	Hour	Summary of Events and Information	Remarks and references to Appendices
I.29.K.0.3.	26/9/18		The Battery paraded at 11.30 a.m. Marched to the line taken over from the 620 KMB. Rear Hqrs / reserved at I.29.K.0.3. WS.	
BATTERY HQRS. Q.15.d.8.5.	27/9/18		Enemy T.M. inactive. Work carried out on both new positions for 1 and 2 guns. Small improvements carried out in other emplacements. 250 rounds of ammunition carried forward to guns on left sector. WS.	
"	28/9/18		Enemy T.M. quiet. Work continued on new gun emplacements and clearing and assembling ammunition. 720 rounds were taken to a forward dump. WS.	
"	29/9/18		Enemy T.M. quiet. Work continued on new gun emplacements and assembling ammunition. WS.	
"	30/9/18		A large number of aeroplane bombs were dropped on Q.15.d between 9 pm & 11 pm. Enemy T.M.s inactive. Orders received for the Bde to be relieved by the 123rd Infantry Bde on the night and 127 Infantry on left. WS.	Battery Orders No 54.
"	1/10/18		Battery Orders issued for the relief. WS.	Battery Orders No 55.

WAR DIARY
or
INTELLIGENCE SUMMARY.

(Erase heading not required.)

Army Form C. 2118.

Place	Date	Hour	Summary of Events and Information	Remarks and references to Appendices
Q.14.k.8.5.	26/9/18		The Battery moved into position with ammunition to right guns were withdrawn to meet positions in order to bombard CANAL WOOD SWITCH and DERBY TRENCH during the barrage. The right and left attacks	
"	27/9/18		The 9th & 19th Div: in conjunction with the Prussians on the right and left attacked the enemy trenches in the HINDENBURG LINE. During the barrage commencing 7.52am our mortars fired 280 rounds on to trenches in the HINDENBURG LINE.	
"	28/9/18		The Battery concentrated at Falleng Fell at 6pm. Men rested during the day.	
Q.14.k.2.6.	29/9/18		General cleaning up. Battery Wagon moved to Q.14.k.2.6. 2 O.R. admitted to S.D. Pont.	
"	30/9/18		General fatigues. General cleaning up.	

F.A.N.[?]
Lieut
O.C. 126 TM Battery

War Diary

126th Light Trench Mortar Battery.

Volume XX

From Oct 1st 1918 to Oct 31st 1918.

Army Form C. 2118.

WAR DIARY
or
INTELLIGENCE SUMMARY.
(Erase heading not required.)

Instructions regarding War Diaries and Intelligence Summaries are contained in F. S. Regs., Part II. and the Staff Manual respectively. Title pages will be prepared in manuscript.

Place	Date	Hour	Summary of Events and Information	Remarks and references to Appendices
HARINCOURT WOOD Q.14.K.2.6.	11/9/18		The day spent in cleaning up equipment, Camp fatigues & Recreational training.	
"	12/9/18		Ceremonial parade in the morning. Inspection of Medal ribbons by Divisional Commander. Offr. strength 14 O.R. strength 101 The M.S.M. ribbon. The afternoon devoted to Recreational training. Hygiene lecture. 1 O.R. rejoined from leave.	
			The continental system of time i.e. the 24 hour clock brought into use throughout British Army.	
"	13/9/18		Training for the morning consists of Physical Repair training and Gun Drill. In the afternoon Recreational Games. Hygiene lecture. 1 O.R. rejoined from leave.	
"	14/9/18		Daily training programme carried out consisting of Gun Drill and Gas helmet Movement. Instructional Lecture by Capt. Morlaise. Sports and Refresher lectures in the afternoon.	

Army Form C. 2118.

WAR DIARY
or
INTELLIGENCE SUMMARY.
(Erase heading not required.)

Place	Date	Hour	Summary of Events and Information	Remarks and references to Appendices
HARRICOURT Wood (U.5.2.6.)	5/10/18		Daily training programme carried out consists of Physical & Bayonet training. Map Reading & various tactical exercises of gun positions, gun laying by compass. 2 O.R.'s proceeded on 14 days leave to U.K. Winter time came into use from midnight 5/6th Sept 18. JM	
"	6/10/18		The Battery paraded for Divine Service. The Batts at RUYAUCOURT attempted to shell the factory in the afternoon. JM	
"	7/10/18		Training for the day consists of Physical & Bayonet training, foot & mounted drill, tactical exercise. Orders received for the Battery to be prepared to move forward by 9pm on 8 inst. Battery Orders issued for the move. JM	
"	8/10/18		The Battery paraded & marched to LAVACQUERIE. Rear pages moves from REMICOURT to vicinity of BEAUCAMP. JM The Battery moved forward to BRISEUX WOOD (N10 c.0.8.) JM	Battery Order No. 68

Army Form C. 2118.

WAR DIARY
or
INTELLIGENCE SUMMARY.
(Erase heading not required.)

Instructions regarding War Diaries and Intelligence Summaries are contained in F. S. Regs., Part II. and the Staff Manual respectively. Title pages will be prepared in manuscript.

Place	Date	Hour	Summary of Events and Information	Remarks and references to Appendices
BRISEUX WOOD (N.10.c.0.5)	10/10/18		Rear Hqrs rejoined the Battery. The Bay spent in the cleaning & renewal of equipment. The Bdr. en route to N.5 Cerisier. Orders received for the move to FONTAINE-AU-PIRE. Battery orders issued for the move.	Battery Order Nº 66
FONTAINE AU-PIRE	11/10/18		The Battery formed at eighteen minutes to eighteen o'clock. Night of 12/13 quiet. Battery order issued for the move to AULICOURT FARM.	Battery Order No. 67
	13/10/18		Orders received for the Bk to relieve the N.Z. Div on the line at AULICOURT FARM. The move postponed for 1½ hours. The Battery formed at 2330 hrs and marched to AULICOURT FARM and took over billets. The Brigade now in support to the 137 Inf Bde. No troops on line to U.K.	
AULICOURT FARM	13/10/18		Battery rested during the day. Lieut. Rejoined the Battery from leave.	
"	14/10/18			

Army Form C. 2118.

WAR DIARY
or
INTELLIGENCE SUMMARY.
(Erase heading not required.)

Instructions regarding War Diaries and Intelligence Summaries are contained in F. S. Regs., Part II. and the Staff Manual respectively. Title pages will be prepared in manuscript.

Place	Date	Hour	Summary of Events and Information	Remarks and references to Appendices
AULICOURT FARM.	12/10/18		Training for the day consisted of Physical Bayonet training Gas Drill & Recreational training in the afternoon. JH	
	13/10/18		The morning spent on Physical Bayonet training, cleaning guns. Recreational training in the afternoon. P.M. Parades as usual. JH	
"	14/10/18		Training for the day consisted of Bayonet Drill, Musketry, Physical Bayonet training. JH	
"	15/10/18		7:00 parades at gun to entrain practice of the attack. Operation orders received for the relief of the 125th Bde by the 76th Bde. Battery orders issued for the relief of 75th RMA. JH	Battery Order No. 168.
PROYELLE.	16/10/18		The Battery proceeds to Proyelle at 8 a.m. Advance party proceeds to Ayre 128 R.M.A. to take over billets. The Battery parades at 2 p.m. & marches to new lines and took over from the 75th R.M.A. Relief completed by 4:30 p.m. Orders issued for the attack.	Battery Order Nos. 169 & 170.

WAR DIARY or INTELLIGENCE SUMMARY

Army Form C. 2118.

Place	Date	Hour	Summary of Events and Information	Remarks and references to Appendices
GRAVELLE	19/10/18		Attended C.O.'s Conference at Brigade H.Qrs. at noon. Operation and Administration Orders issued for the resumption of the advance. Information received Recent movement [harasses] at 5.0 p.m. and proceeded to the line.	Battery Order No. 71 and 72.
"	20/10/18		The Battery resumed the advance. The 197th Div. in conjunction with Divisions on the right and left attacked the enemy position. The 116th Bde. was the leading Brigade. 1 Section of Battery was allotted to the C.O. ready for the operation. Zero hour was 2.0 p.m. The attack took place in thick rain. The enemy fought on all objectives were taken up & several tram lines were captured. At 9.0 p.m. the 197th Bde. was ordered to push through to the [line] of the railway 1 km. eastwards. The new line was reached for the evening, 1 of our armies moved [from] -	
"	21/10/18			
AULNOURT FARM	27/10/18		The 197 Infantry relieved the 136 Infantry Brigade in [the relief] of the Battery by the 183 Divl Artillery. On completion of relief the Battery marched to Aulnourt Farm and took over billets.	Battery Order No. 73

Army Form C. 2118.

WAR DIARY
or
INTELLIGENCE SUMMARY.
(Erase heading not required.)

Instructions regarding War Diaries and Intelligence Summaries are contained in F. S. Regs., Part II. and the Staff Manual respectively. Title pages will be prepared in manuscript.

Place	Date	Hour	Summary of Events and Information	Remarks and references to Appendices
AUTICOURT FARM	23/10/16		The day devoted to cleaning up and preparation for the Battery's move to BEAUVOIS. Battery orders issued.	Battery Orders No. 92
BEAUVOIS	24/10/16		The Battery paraded at 10.30 and moved to BEAUVOIS and took over billets. I OR rejoined the Battery from leave.	
"	25/10/16		The day spent in an attempt to put the Battery lines & billets in order. Harness inspected by the Bty Sergt Major. The Battery paraded at 2.00 p.m. for stables. I OR rejoins the Battery from leave.	
"	26/10/16		Training for the day consisted of Gun Drill Gun and Harness Drill. Refresher lecture.	
"	27/10/16		Training for the day consists of Rimo Drill Battery Drill Refresher lectures. Recreational training in the afternoon.	
"	28/10/16		Daily training programme carried out Lunch & gun troubles to the officer 3rd Echelon PARIS PLAGE for a weeks rest.	

WAR DIARY
or
INTELLIGENCE SUMMARY.

Army Form C. 2118.

Place	Date	Hour	Summary of Events and Information	Remarks and references to Appendices
BEAUVOIS	29/4/18		Training. With 294 Brigade (Range Practice). Maps for hand book of Brigade Lecture. 1 OR taken on the strength of the Battery to complete establishment. Sergt H. Roberson to Hospital. (Left knee) dated 29/4/18.	
"	30/4		The Battery paraded at 9pm for an hour. 4 OR proceeded on 14 days leave to UK.	
"	1/4/18		Ceremonial parade in the morning. The Divisional Commander Major Gen. T. Marsden bid Champion M.C. Presented 2 Military Cross ribbons. 1 OR 3 years service good.	

J H Ceumpton M.C. Capt.
OC 126. L.T.M Battery.

126th Light Trench Mortar Battery.

War Diary

Volume XXI

From 1st Novr 1918 to 30th Novr 1918.

Army Form C. 2118.

WAR DIARY
or
INTELLIGENCE-SUMMARY.
(Erase heading not required.)

Place	Date	Hour	Summary of Events and Information	Remarks and references to Appendices
BEAUVOIS	1/11/18		Training for the day consisted of Musketry and Battery Drill. War Diary for the month of Oct sent to Bde. JWN	
"	2/11/18		The Battery paraded for Musketry for one and Drill & Training through the Masters & NCOs provided by the Junior NCOs class at Sappers Camp. Warning order received to be prepared to move on the night of 3rd/4th Nos. JWN	
"	3/11/18		Brigade Order No 5 received for the continuation of the advance. Battery Order issued for the move to SOLESMES and BEAUDIGNIES. 2 OR proceeded on leave to UK. 1 OR rejoined from leave. 1 NCO proceeded to the 37th Corps Gas School. The Battery paraded at 1845 hours and marched to SOLESMES and took over billets. JWN	Battery Orders No. 75
SOLESMES	4/11/18		1 OR proceeded to both TM school The Battery paraded at 1300 hours and marched to BEAUDIGNIES and took over billets. Bde Karamy reported that the Bde will probably move forward early on the 5th Nov. Brigade Orders No 6 & 7 received. JWN	

WAR DIARY or INTELLIGENCE SUMMARY

Army Form C. 2118.

Place	Date	Hour	Summary of Events and Information	Remarks and references to Appendices
BEAUDIGNIES	5/11/18		1st Bn BEAUDIGNIES and marched to HERBIGNIES under weather conditions amounting there at mid-word. The march was then continued into FOREST DE MORMAL to point of assembly. From there orders to join the two forward battalions, to advance. The second Bn was ordered to 1st Mk to Regt and in conformation to the 1st Bn already. Both sections encountered great difficulty moving to had made orders and the undergrowth of the forest. Hindrance had little movement at FORESTER'S HOUSE South and all movement and guns were landed a distance of 1000 yds to point of assembly. Rain fell incessantly and the wind were in a treeless condition.	
"	6/11/18	N.20.a.4.3.	The Bn. commenced the advance at 06.30 hours and encountered heavy M.G. fire. The tall heath was then to 300 yds on up of the advance of the 6th 2nd. To pushed on to the left forward for great hostile machinery of fallen timber to engage E.M.G. but could not get within range. From this onwards the advance was continued to Père des Pierrot between advancing with the forward Coy of 18th East Kents R. but little M.G. fire was experienced. Newport continued.	
"	7/11/18	O.3.d.K.3.8.	Heavy M.G. secured to O.3d.K.3.8. The advance continued to the outskirts of NEUVILLE, which was eventually captured by the 1st Manchester Bn. 18th East Kents moved to support with the patrols of 1st East Kent R and 1st Mk to patrols of 1st Manchester Regt. Few trees reported, the Brigade covering the day.	Battery order 10/9

WAR DIARY or INTELLIGENCE SUMMARY.

Army Form C. 2118.

Place	Date	Hour	Summary of Events and Information	Remarks and references to Appendices
Hautmont	9/11/18		The Battery proceeded to HAUTMONT and took over billets. 1 O.R. proceeded on leave to U.K. Signal Order No 10 received. OO/A	
"	10/11/18		Day spent in cleaning up. O/A	
"	11/11/16		Hostilities ceased at 1100 hours. The day spent in cleaning up. O/A.	
"	12/11/18		Were showing the terms of the armistice received. Day spent in cleaning up. 71969. L/Cpl Leare. C. & 71101110. Bdr Robertson. R. ? promoted Corporals. OO/A. Lodge.	
"	13/11/18		Training for the day consisted of Rifle Inspection & Rifle Inspection. Recreational training in the afternoon. OO/A	
"	14/11/18		Training carried out consisted of Inspections, Physical training. OO/A	

Army Form C. 2118.

WAR DIARY
or
INTELLIGENCE SUMMARY.
(Erase heading not required.)

Instructions regarding War Diaries and Intelligence Summaries are contained in F.S. Regs., Part II. and the Staff Manual respectively. Title pages will be prepared in manuscript.

Place	Date	Hour	Summary of Events and Information	Remarks and references to Appendices
HAUTMONT	14/11/18		Cont. Squad Drill, Ceremonial Drill and Musketry	
"	15/11/18		2. O.R. proceeded on 14 days leave to U.K. DN. The Battery paraded at 0900 for Route March. Short in the afternoon. DN.	
"	16/11/18		Parades cancelled owing to the Ceremonial presentation of the Guns captured by the 4th Middx Regt to the Maire and Citizens of HAUTMONT. DN.	
"	17/11/18		Church parade cancelled owing to a lecture being given on Demobilization by an Officer from G.H.Q. 1 O.R. reported from leave. DN.	
"	18/11/18		Parades for the day consisted of Inspection, Ceremonial Drill, Arms Drill & Battery Drill. To men of the Battery inoculated. Fourth Army Standing Orders Resumed. DN.	

Army Form C. 2118.

WAR DIARY
or
INTELLIGENCE SUMMARY.
(Erase heading not required.)

Instructions regarding War Diaries and Intelligence Summaries are contained in F. S. Regs., Part II. and the Staff Manual respectively. Title pages will be prepared in manuscript.

Place	Date	Hour	Summary of Events and Information	Remarks and references to Appendices
HAMMOND	19/11/16		½ Parade every to inoculation. JM	
"	20/11/16		½ Parade every to inoculation JM	
"	21/11/16		Training for the day consists of Inspection, Gunnery Drill, Arms Drill & Battery Drill. JM	
			1. OR returns from leave JM	
"	22/11/16		Parades for the day, Inspection & Route March. JM	
			1. OR returns from leave JM	
"	23/11/16		Training for the day consists of Inspection Gunns Drill, Musketry.	
			4. OR's rejoined the Battery from leave.	
			1. OR admitted sick to H.t.	
			1. OR. Struck off Strength on being transferred to CCS. JM	

A7092I. Wt. W12839/M1297. 750,000. 1/17. D. D & L., Ltd. Forms/C2118/14.

Army Form C. 2118.

WAR DIARY
or
INTELLIGENCE SUMMARY.
(Erase heading not required.)

Instructions regarding War Diaries and Intelligence Summaries are contained in F. S. Regs., Part II. and the Staff Manual respectively. Title pages will be prepared in manuscript.

Place	Date	Hour	Summary of Events and Information	Remarks and references to Appendices
HAVRINCOURT	26/11/18		Voluntary Church services. JM	
	26/11/18		Training for the day consisted of Squad Drill, Musketry, Battery Drill. The Battery paraded for bath at Bertincourt. 1. O.R. rejoined the Battery from Field Ambulance. JM	
	27/11/18		Daily Training programme carried out. 355558 Cpl Heighton. D.R. M.S.M. } awarded the Military Medal 377006 - Fisher. Ta. JM	
	27/11/18		The Battery paraded at 0825 hours for Brigade Route March. 2 O.R's proceeded on leave to U.K. JM	
	28/11/18		The Battery paraded at 10.45 hours for inspection by the Brigade Commander. Battery Officers Mess, Orderly Room, Stores and O.M. Stores were also inspected. JM	

A7092¹. Wt. w12839/M1297. 750,000. 1/17. D. D & L. Ltd. Forms/C2118/14.

WAR DIARY
or
INTELLIGENCE SUMMARY.
(Erase heading not required.)

Army Form C. 2118.

Place	Date	Hour	Summary of Events and Information	Remarks and references to Appendices
MAUTMORT	29/11/18		The Battery paraded at 0815 hours for Brigade Route March. 1 O.R. taken on strength of the Battery to complete establishment. JM	Battery Order 10.2.19
"	30/11/18		Training for the day consisted of Irun Drive, Battery Drill. Battery Orders issued in connection with the visit of His Majesty the King to the Fourth Army Area. JM	

J.M. Alexander. Capt
O.C. 126. 27th Battery.

Operation Order No 75.

(1) On the night of the 3rd/4th inst the Battery will move to SOLESMES VIA JEUNE BOIS – BETHENCOURT – VIESLEY – BRIASTRE – BELLEVUE – SOLESMES.

(2) Starting point will be road junction west of JEUNE BOIS I.11.b.3.8.

(3) On the 4th Nov Battery will move to BEAUDIGNIES VIA VERTIGNEUL track W 23 b 91 – W.18.b.4.2. – PONT A PIERRAS – BEAUDIGNIES.

(4) Billeting parties will report to the Staff Capt at SOLESMES and BEAUDIGNIES respectively in advance of the Column.

(5) Watches will be synchronized at 1700 hours on the 3rd Nov and 1000 hours on the 4th Nov at Brigade Hqrs.

(6) Brigade Hqrs will close at BEAUVOIS at 1845 hours on the 3rd Nov after which hour all reports will be sent to the head of the Column.

(7) On arrival at each destination a runner will immediately report to Brigade Hqrs notifying Bde Hqrs of the location of the Battery.

(8) 100 yards will be maintained between units and companies. Halts will take place at 10 minutes before each clock hour.

(9) Battery will be ready to move off at 1850 hrs for the move of the 3rd/4th Nov.

(10) Orders as regards transport available have been issued.

(11) Refilling point for the 4th Nov SOLESMES.

Signed H.T. HAMPSON
Capt
O.C. 126 L.T.M Battery

3/11/18

Operation Order No. 76.

Battery Hqrs will move tomorrow to LA HAUTE RUE O.33.d

All transport will move with Battery Hqrs and will be prepared to move off at 0700 hours.

Signed H.T. HAMPSON
Capt
7/11/18.   O.C. 126th T.M. Battery

Battery Order No 97.

1. His Majesty the King will visit the Fourth Army Area on Decr 8th 1918.
2. Every facility will be given for employed men to attend the parade.
3. The Battery will parade outside the Officers Mess at 0900 hours. Dress: - Walking out dress/Slacks belts with side arms
4. The starting point for the Brigade will be Railway Level Crossing at P.32.d.9.7 and the Battery will pass this point at 0923 hours.
5. Route. P.23.d.2.0. - Q.13.d.1.1. - Q.19.b.7.5. - LES GRAVETTES.
6. A parade state showing actual strength on parade will be handed in to Orderly Room by 0900 hours 1 Decr

               Signed H.T. Hampson Capt

30/11/18   OC 126. R.M.B.

126th Light Trench Mortar Battery

War Diary

Volume XXII

From Decr. 1st 1918 to Decr. 31st 1918

Army Form C. 2118.

WAR DIARY
or
INTELLIGENCE SUMMARY.
(Erase heading not required.)

Instructions regarding War Diaries and Intelligence Summaries are contained in F.S. Regs., Part II. and the Staff Manual respectively. Title pages will be prepared in manuscript.

Place	Date	Hour	Summary of Events and Information	Remarks and references to Appendices
HAVRINCOURT	1/1/18		A.M. The Kg. relieved the Fourth Bring Rees. The Brigade proceeded by road, route to LES GRATETTES via the main HAVRINCOURT - HARBEUGE Road, and were employed by the Bayonets. O.R. taken over bar to the men.	
"	2/1/18		Spent the day composed of Inspection. Uniform Drill. Musketry (Range Practice) & R. of course the Battery from Leave. Evacuated to B.C.H. and struck off the strength of the Battery.	
			Training (Coy) amount morning of Speech & trench Bill and Drill. Musketry, trench several out. 1 O.R. returned to school.	
"	3/1/18		These received concerning Brigade Route Marel owing to bad weather. 1 O.R. returned from Leave 1 O.R. taken on strength of the Battery being complete establishment.	

WAR DIARY
INTELLIGENCE SUMMARY

Army Form C. 2118.

Place	Date	Hour	Summary of Events and Information	Remarks and references to Appendices
HAVINCOURT	3/9/16		The Battery paraded in full marching order at 10:15 am for Brigade Route March. No more of note. Attended lecture of reference? the gallant front lines.	
"	4/9/16		Training for the day consisted of Infantry Squad Drill Musketry, Range Practice, Gun drill & Lectures.	
"	5/9/16		Ordinary orders received for the men & checked down. Warning Order for the day consisted of Gas Drill & Battery Drill. 1st Gun Sub squad moved to at 7:30 at Gun School.	
"	6/9/16		Preliminary Demonstration Morning. Recreation events afternoon. On Bye Parade in deep lines at 6 P.M.	
"	7/9/16		The Battery paraded at 9:00 in full marching order for route march. On return to billets executed & out struck of the strength of the Battery.	

Army Form C. 2118.

WAR DIARY
or
INTELLIGENCE SUMMARY.

(Erase heading not required.)

Instructions regarding War Diaries and Intelligence Summaries are contained in F. S. Regs., Part II. and the Staff Manual respectively. Title pages will be prepared in manuscript.

Place	Date	Hour	Summary of Events and Information	Remarks and references to Appendices
HOUDAIN	19/2/16		The Battery paraded for Ceremonial Drill. Runs Drill Semaphore signalling. 1 OR reported to the Depot for duty. 17/16 men on sick. 10 at Depot. Riding Instruction for NCO's & men commenced who do not know how to ride. JH	
"	20/2/16		Paraded for the morning exercise of Horses. Drew Harness 1. OR Rejoined from Hospital. Brigade Orders received for Division to move to GUZI. JH	
"	21/2/16		Paraded for the morning exercise of Horses. Brigade Orders No 78 received for the move. 1 OR Rejoined the Battery from hire. Proceeded onto Billeting Party. JH	Brigade order No 78
"	22/2/16		The Battery paraded at 9.30 a.m. for departure. JH	

Army Form C. 2118.

WAR DIARY
or
INTELLIGENCE SUMMARY.
(Erase heading not required.)

Place	Date	Hour	Summary of Events and Information	Remarks and references to Appendices
HAUMONT	14/4/19		The Battery paraded at 08.30 hrs and marched to LAMORIES. Arrived there at 14.15 hrs and took over billets. The men fell out on the line of march. Lt. Bradbury and NCO proceeded in advance to BINCHE to arrange billets. JN	
LAMORIES	15/4/19		The Battery paraded at 08.00 hrs and marched to BINCHE. Arrived there at 13.30 hrs and took over billets. No man fell out on line of march. Lt. Pairson 11/05 proceeded in advance to FONTAINE L'EVEQUE to arrange billets. JN	
BINCHE	16/4/19		The Battery paraded at 08.30 hrs and marched to FONTAINE L'EVEQUE. 1 O.R. admitted to Hosp. JN arriving there at 11.45 hrs.	
FONTAINE L'EVEQUE	17/4/19		Rifle Inspection at 10.30 hrs. Remainder of the morning spent in cleaning equipment etc. Rest in the afternoon. JN	
"	19/4/19		The Battery paraded at 08.15 hrs and marched to GILLY and took over billets. Men rested in the afternoon. JN	

WAR DIARY

Army Form C. 2118.

Place	Date	Hour	Summary of Events and Information	Remarks and references to Appendices
GILLN	19/1/18		The day spent on usual fatigues during experience 1 & 2. JN	
"	20/1/18		The Battery paraded at 0930 hrs for fatigues. 1 OR evacuated to cas. & unit M.D. as sick of the Battery. JN	
"	21/1/18		The Battery paraded at 0930 hrs for Inspection. General Drill Signal & Educational training. JN	
"	22/1/18		The Battery turned to Divine Service at 0930 hrs for Service. ex Concert held "9th East Lancs Regt." JN	
"	23/1/18		The Battery turned at 0930 hrs for inspection. Remainder of morning spent in fatigues. 1 OR proceeded to England for demobilization. JN	
"	24/1/18		Battery on general fatigues in the morning. Lecture at 1500 hrs on forecast the "1st East Rang R" on "How to know foreign languages". 1 OR proceeded on 18 days leave to U.K. (inclusive of days Rys. travel) 2 OR taken on strength of the complete establishment. JN	

Army Form C. 2118.

WAR DIARY
~~INTELLIGENCE SUMMARY.~~
(Erase heading not required.)

Instructions regarding War Diaries and Intelligence Summaries are contained in F. S. Regs. Part II. and the Staff Manual respectively. Title pages will be prepared in manuscript.

Place	Date	Hour	Summary of Events and Information	Remarks and references to Appendices
GILLY	25/1/19		General Holiday. 1 OR proceeded to England for demobilization. JN	
"	26/1/19		General Holiday. 1 OR proceeded on 14 days leave to U.K. JN	
"	27/1/19		Battery paraded at 09.30 hrs for inspection. Lecture at 10.00 hrs at CAFE ROYAL (3 CHAUSSE de CHARLEROI) Subject "AUSTRIA" Lieut E. Pratt rejoined the Battery from leave JN	
"	28/1/19		The Battery paraded at 09.15 hrs for inspection JN	
"	29/1/19		A. Battery paraded for divine service in the drawn enclosure eastwards at 10.00 hrs JN	
"	30/1/19		General programme for the morning consisted of Inspections, Guard Mount, Foot drill and Arms drill. JN	

Army Form C. 2118.

WAR DIARY
or
INTELLIGENCE SUMMARY.
(Erase heading not required.)

Instructions regarding War Diaries and Intelligence Summaries are contained in F. S. Regs., Part II. and the Staff Manual respectively. Title pages will be prepared in manuscript.

Place	Date	Hour	Summary of Events and Information	Remarks and references to Appendices
GHQ	30/6		Training for the day consisted of Battalion Gymnasium Drill. Gas Drill. Bomb Drill.	

W. J. Thompson Col.
O.C. 26 Kimberley

Battery Order No. 78

1. The Battery commencing on 14th inst will march to CHARLEROI Area.
2. The move will take place in stages with one days rest on 17th inst. at FONTAINE-L'EVEQUE.
3. The Battery will march immediately in rear of Brigade HQ.
4. All transport will accompany the Battery on the line of march.
5. Dress. Drill order, with caps.
6. March Discipline. No man will be allowed to fall out without a chit signed by an officer. All stragglers capable of marching will be brought on by the rear party.
7. Marching out strengths will be forwarded to Bde HQ by 0800 hours on each day of the march (Returns of the number who fall out will be rendered to BHQ by 1700 hours on the day of the march. Nil returns will be rendered.

8. The Billeting party sent in advance will be under orders of the Staff Captain, and will arrange to meet the Battery on its arrival at each fresh billeting area.

9. The billeting party will ascertain the location of Brigade HQ, but in the event of permanent Bde HQ not having been fixed by the time of arrival of the Battery the Staff Captain will so notify billeting parties. In this case temporary report centres will be established as follows:-

  14th Decr. Opposite GRAND RENG CHURCH
  15th " Main Road Junction, ¼ mile NE of E in BINCHE
  16th " FONTAINE L'EVEQUE CHURCH

10. Location of Battery Hqrs will be notified to BHQ on completion of each move. The positions of such Hqrs will be clearly marked by notice boards, immediately on arrival.

11. A watch will be sent by Bde Signals on the evening of the day prior to each days march. Watches will, in addition be checked with the Brigade Major on passing the starting point.
12. March table is hereby attached.

[signature] Capt.

12/12/18   O.C. 126. L.T.M.B.

March Table

Starting point

Date	Unit	Time	Place	Route	Destination
14/11/18	176 Bom B.	0900 hrs	Rd Junction ½ mile S. of L. in NEUF MESNIL	Sous le Bois - MAUBEUGE. VIEUX RENG.	LAMERIES.
15/11/18	-do-	0900 hrs	Rd Junction ¼ Mile N. of R. in GRAND RENG STA	Cross Roads ½ mile S of G. in GIVRY-ESTINNE AU MONT	BINCHE.
16/11/18	-do-	0907 hrs	Cross Roads 150 yds S.W. of T. in TRIEU	MAIN MONS - CHARLEROI Rd	FONTAINE L'EVEQUE
18/11/18	-do-	0900 hrs	Cross Roads ½ mile S. of G. in GOUTROUX	Main BINCHE - CHARLEROI Rd - Cross Rd 400 yds S of V. in DAMPREMY - Road Junction 300 yds W. of B. in BROUSSETENRE	GILLY.

Administrative Instructions issued
with Battery Order No. 78

1. Billeting. The Billeting area for each
day is shown on attached table.
Special attention will be taken that
all billets are left in a clean
and sanitary condition. In all
probability, no rear parties will
be left.
 An advance billeting party
consisting of 1 Officer & 1 N.C.O. will
report to D.H.Q. HAZEBROUCK at
10.00 hours on the 13th inst. By horse
transport will be carried. The same
for the 14th day & subsequent days
will be notified later to the officer's
in charge of billeting party.
 Special attention is directed to
rates of billeting in Belgium.

2. Transport. 1. G.S. Waggon and
2 L.S. Waggons will be rideable.
1 G.S. will be loaded with 100 rounds
of ammunition and 2 guns.

A guide will be sent to direct the 2 S. Lieuts. from D.P.C. on evening of the 13th inst.

Transport will remain throughout the march. Men and animals will be rationed up to Dec 14th inclusive, from which date transport personnel and animals will be taken on strength of the Battery. On last day of march transport will rejoin HQrs of their own unit.

3. Refilling will be as follows:—
Supply waggons will refill at 07.30 hours daily. A guide will be detached to meet supply waggons on each day.

    15. Dec   ROUVROY.
    16. "   BINCHE (Western Edge of)
    17. "   FONTAINE L'EVEQUE
                (East E of EVEQUE.)
    18 "   FONTAINE L'EVEQUE
                (East E of EVEQUE.)

4. Fuel. Sufficient coal will be carried for 16th & 17th inst. On the 18th & 19th inst coal may be drawn from the dump at ANDERHAUS.
5. Packs. Will be carried on handcarts. Jerkins will be included in the packs.
6. D.P.D.O.S. will be located at CHARLEROI from the 14th inst.
7. Leave parties. During the march men proceeding on leave will proceed to the Refilling Point arriving there by 1800 hours at which hour lorries will leave.

A.J. Army Capt.

12/12/18   OC. 126. L.T.M.B.

Billeting Area.

Date	Unit	Place	
14/15ᵗʰ	126. L.T.M.B.	LAMORIES.	(a)
15/16	-do-	BINCHE. (W. end of Town.)	(a)
16/17ᵗʰ	-do-	FONTAINE L'EVEQUE.	(a)
17/18ᵗʰ	-do-	No change.	
18/19ᵗʰ	-do-	GILLY.	(b)

(a) Billets from Mairie.
(b) " " Town Major.

www.ingramcontent.com/pod-product-compliance
Lightning Source LLC
Chambersburg PA
CBHW080856230426
43662CB00013B/2117